other books by the Trobisches:

*Better Is Your Love Than Wine*
*An Experience of Love*
*I Loved a Girl*
*I Married You*
*The Joy of Being a Woman*
*Living with Unfulfilled Desires*
*Love Is a Feeling to Be Learned*
*Love Yourself*
*My Beautiful Feeling*
*On Our Way Rejoicing*

booklets by Walter Trobisch:

*Martin Luther's Quiet Time*
*Spiritual Dryness*

Walter Trobisch

# The Misunderstood Man

## Why Men Suffer & What Can Be Done About It

InterVarsity Press
Downers Grove
Illinois 60515

InterVarsity Press is the book-publishing division of Inter-Varsity Christian Fellowship, a student movement active on campus at hundreds of universities, colleges and schools of nursing. For information about local and regional activities, write IVCF, 233 Langdon St., Madison, WI 53703.

Distributed in Canada through InterVarsity Press, 860 Denison St., Unit 3, Markham, Ontario L3R 4H1, Canada.

Acknowledgment is made for permission to use the following copyrighted material:

From Goethe's Faust, Parts I and II, translated by Louis MacNeice. Copyright 1951, 1954 by Frederick Louis MacNeice; renewed 1979 by Hedli MacNeice. Reprinted by permission of Oxford University Press, Inc., New York, and Faber and Faber Ltd., London.

From "Das Tagebuch" Goethes und Rilkes "Sieben Gedichte." Walter Trobisch's adapted translation is used by permission of Insel Verlag, Frankfurt.

From Ausgewählte Werke in zwei Bänden by Kurt Tucholsky. Walter Trobisch's adapted translation is used by permission of Rowoht Verlag, Reinbek bei Hamburg.

From A Growing Love by Ulrich Schaffer. Used by permission of Harper & Row, New York.

Cover illustration: Michael Conway

ISBN 0-87784-302-3

Printed in the United States of America

**Library of Congress Cataloging in Publication Data**
Trobisch, Walter.
    The misunderstood man.

    Bibliography: p.
    1. Men—Psychology.    2. Men—Attitudes.    3. Men—
Religious life.    4. Sex role.    I. Title.
HQ1090.T76        1983            305.3'1              83-6110
ISBN 0-87784-302-3

| 16 | 15 | 14 | 13 | 12 | 11 | 10 | 9 | 8 | 7 | 6 | 5 | 4 | 3 | 2 |
|----|----|----|----|----|----|----|----|----|----|----|----|----|----|----|
| 95 | 94 | 93 | 92 | 91 | 90 | 89 | 88 | 87 | 86 | 85 | 84 | | | |

## Foreword

"Man is suffering, but woman don't know it." I once saw these words painted on a small bus in Accra, Ghana. Perhaps this is the essence of what Walter wants to say in this book. He talked more about it to his friends and me than about any other book which came from his pen.

The unfinished manuscript lay on his desk at the time of his sudden death, October 13, 1979. The first two chapters were written in his generous longhand with notes on the margin to be included in his second draft. The final section, "The Free Man," was found only in skeleton form—like the bare bones of a tree in winter which give us only the form of how beautiful the tree would be in spring, summer and fall.

The last part of the book is the answer to the first two.

After we read of how a man suffers and how he reacts to his hurt, we read of the man set free to be a man—the redeemed man. He is healed of his wounds, made whole. He has accepted himself, his strengths as well as his weaknesses because he knows he has been accepted by the heavenly Father.

I've often asked young people whether they know a freed man, a redeemed man. Most of them shake their heads sadly and say, "I know none." I asked the same question of an older woman who said: "I don't know any either—only those who are on the way to becoming redeemed men. Walter was one of them."

Walter had the courage for the provisional, for the temporary. I found this sentence in his notes for an epilog to this book: "It belongs to being redeemed—to be satisfied with the provisional, the temporary. Even if one never reaches the goal, it is good to be going in the right direction. . . . It is not my intention to give the last word on men in this book. Those who are only satisfied if they can write the last word will never write anything."

It is in this spirit that we share the next to the last of Walter Trobisch. May it help men to better understand and accept themselves. May it help wives to better understand their husbands.

*Ingrid Trobisch*

## Acknowledgment

Acknowledgment is due the very important work of Walter's best friend, Pastor Wolfgang Caffier, who helped me to decipher the marginal notes and to put together the pieces. My son David also edited the first draft, making "all the words stand up straight," and removing repetition. I am deeply grateful to the staff of InterVarsity Press for bringing this unborn child to birth.

*Ingrid Trobisch*

### The Typical Man: A Lament

*Kurt Tucholsky*

The typical man
     *man*
       *man—*
He's the misunderstood man.
He has a car, a job, a home and a position.
He has a bank account for food, gas and tuition.
He also has his opinion, contra or pro,
And even has a wife,
but this he may not know.
He calls her "Mommy" or "Baby"
with a smile and happy pat.
He's a man and that is that.
He's the self-sufficient man
 who feels that a woman will never
 quite understand him—ever.

The typical man
     *man*
       *man—*
He's the misunderstood man.
His wife lies beside him as he snores in his bed
wishing he'd be just a little gentle instead.
But he thinks: Is she not my wife?
Does she want more out of life?
He has no need to be needed.
He feels completely completed.
He bought her a dress and a hat.
He is a man—and that is that.
He's the self-sufficient man
 who feels that a woman will never
 quite understand him—ever.

*The typical man*
                *man*
                        *man—*
*He's the misunderstood man.*
*He does not try to court his wife.*
*There are more important things in life.*
*It's up to her, whatever his mood,*
*to do his laundry and cook his food.*
*The main thing is she obeys his will.*
*If not, he could have another still.*
*And should she doubt his loyalty, then he gets tough:*
*"I am a man and that's enough."*
*He's the self-sufficient man*
  *who feels that a woman will never*
  *quite understand him—ever.*

*The typical man*
                *man*
                        *man—*
*He's the misunderstood man.*
*That's the man who meets his ends,*
*but whom no one understands.*
*He has no need to be needed.*
*He feels completely completed.*
*He feels he's whole and not just half.*
*He is a man—and that's enough.*
  *So being a man makes him feel good,*
  *Except he never feels quite understood.*

Adapted translation by Walter Trobisch

*Prolog*

I first heard Kurt Tucholsky's poem in 1976, forty-five years after it was written, being performed by a cabaret singer. In the tone of her voice the singer expressed all her hostility toward men, thus winning the sure sympathy of the women who were listening. She flung the staccato words "man, man, man" like a drumbeat into the auditorium. Drums! Loud and hard, without concern for sacrifice, without the luxury of violins and flutes and soft, intertwining melodies—*that* is what a man is.

Alas!

Of course, the figure in Tucholsky's lament is a caricature and makes its point by exaggeration. But is there not, as with every exaggeration, a kernel of truth that can only be expressed this way?

It is debatable whether this kernel of truth holds only for the German man or whether it applies to men everywhere and is just more pronounced in the German variety. The path of my life has led me to countries all over the world, and I must confess that I find there is a kernel here that is true for men in general, including me.

Be that as it may, as they read this poem, men involuntarily ask themselves why they feel so misunderstood. If they are truly so self-sufficient and contented, then what torments them so that "a woman will never quite understand"?

In the following pages I would like to offer my thoughts on this question. I could have written a long book about the misunderstood man: there is certainly enough material, and a long book is easier to write than a short one. But would it be read? I suspect that it is hard to get most men to read a long book. And I want my book to be read by as many men as possible.

Years ago my wife wrote a book with the title *The Joy of Being a Woman*. Since then I have felt tempted to write a sequel: *The Pain of Being a Man*. Of course the title is intended humorously. We men do not really have it that bad. But it is interesting, just the same. Much is said and written about the stress and distress borne by women. Their joy, therefore, in being a woman must be strengthened. We men, on the other hand, are usually portrayed as strong and heroic or brutal and oppressive. We must play the role of the strong sex, and, therefore, we need someone to understand us in our weakness. This is exactly what I want to try to do.

I will refer to poets, psychologists and doctors in this book. In the third chapter I will consult the book that has been called the most honest, the truest and the most realistic book in world literature—the Bible. It tells of suffering and defensive men. It also tells of the possibility of living as a freed man, a redeemed man.

Once you have read the book, leave it where your wife is sure to find it. It will do her good too. It will be even better if you talk it over together—better for both of you, better for your understanding of one another.

For all misunderstood men who read this book, my wish is that in the end you will share my conviction that we need not be condemned to a life of being misunderstood.

# *One*
## *The Suffering Man*

# The Insecure Man

Did you ever hear the story about the lawyer who asked one of his fellow attorneys to represent him in a court case? He had worked out his defense, and all his friend had to do was read it at the trial. In the margin at the fourth point he had scribbled, "Raise your voice and pound on the stand when you read this. It's the weakest argument."

Some men do pound their fists on the table to emphasize their points. But mostly they save themselves this effort and instead pound on their accomplishments. In Tucholsky's poem at the beginning of this book, the typical man pounds on his business achievements, on his civic position, on the fact that he has more than done his duty to his wife. Yes, he even bought her a hat. But all these arguments are just as weak as the fourth point of the lawyer's defense.

That's why a man has to pound his fist on the table.

I don't know whether anyone has made a study of all the monuments in the world. Most of those that I have seen depict men. It is mostly men who have been the pioneers, the inventors, the artists, the military heroes, explorers and conquerors. This is a man's role in the theater of the world. This is why he pounds his fist, for in a way he has to be his own monument.

But deep inside, he is really tired of always having to structure, to invent, to conquer. He would rather possess. He would rather have something that stands still, a piece of land that no one will take from him. That is what he would like to have in his marriage too. He is tired of disputing every inch of ground which he has won. He would even like to have God as his partner here because wasn't it through him that he was "joined together" with his wife?

Instead, the roles are reversed. He, the man, the proud conqueror, the monumental figure, has to admit when it comes down to the bare facts that he is dependent upon the woman. He has been on the receiving end since the beginning of his life—and it is the woman who is the giver.

All over the world it is the same story. The one who is on the receiving end always feels inferior, put down in face of the one who gives. The history of world missions shows how developed and not-yet-developed countries are burdened by this. The inferiority complex of those on the receiving end is the main problem in any kind of aid.

This is also true of the help the man receives from the woman in his childhood as well as in his marriage. A child gets security from his mother. She is there for her child and dedicates herself to him. A man would like to have this same security when he is grown. Could it be that *Playboy* magazines and posters of women with naked round breasts, which many men find attractive, are geared to an unconscious and unsatisfied thirst in their lives as infants? Many men find their desire unmanly and even unworthy and can't understand why it has such power over them.

But not only as a child does a man receive more than he gives. His love life is that way too. He would like to think of himself as the Great Lover and as the one who gives. Biologically speaking it looks that way, for he gives his wife seminal fluid. But in reality—in the depths of his being—he feels he is the one who is taking something, the one who is receiving. His wife gives him her body, and he experiences the height of pleasure, climax and then deep relaxation.

Even our language betrays this. A young man thinks he can go out and "get" a girlfriend. He wants to go "steady" with her. A mature man, it is true, "takes" a wife, but he also knows that it is she who "gives herself."

It is this split between our dreams and our real role which gives us men a feeling of uncertainty. That in turn keeps us from living at peace with ourselves. Just as we tend to overlook our wives and their needs, so we pass by ourselves. A woman seeks a man who needs her, who longs for her gifts, who even enjoys being on the receiving end. The one who puts himself in the role of the Great Giver and who, because he is a man, thinks that he is all-sufficient, is only manifesting to the world, with every step he takes, his own inadequacy.

# *The Inadequate Man*

It's all very good, all that a man has to brag about—how hard he works, how he provides for his family, how well he can fix things, yes, even all the committees and organizations he gives his time and money to. But deep down it is never quite enough. His wife affirms him and stands loyally behind him. She even admires him, and yet he feels inadequate. For whatever else she says or does, just by her very being, she is always reminding him of his inadequacy as a man. This is what bothers him and what she can't comprehend.

If he can meet her in a condescending, fatherly manner, calling her his "baby" or his "dear child," then he feels safe. And as a maid, as the one who does his washing and sews on his buttons, she does not make him feel insecure. She also fits into his pattern if she is the source of his pleasure—the one who satisfies his sexual wishes. He can even handle thinking of her as a marriage "object" which he "possesses" like a piece of furniture he has bought. But as a real woman, as a person, she simply doesn't fit into his thinking. She gets in his way, lies diagonally across his path, and he doesn't know what to do with her. "He may also have a wife," as Tucholsky says, "but this he does not know."

"A little tenderness would heal her inner core." But a man doesn't quite believe it. He knows from experience that a huge dose of tenderness is not enough. Yes, when he thinks that he has given her all the tenderness that he can give and his store is depleted, that's just when she's looking for more. At the least expected moment, when he's really feeling good about himself, that's just when she starts to cry—and for no reason at all. It's as if something deep within her is always crying for comfort, and it dawns on him that he will never be able to satisfy completely her deepest longings.

A young doctor came with his wife to talk about their marriage. "We've been married for a year now. I have tried every way that I know to satisfy my wife. But," he sighed, "no matter what I do, I always feel I am inadequate."

The longing of lovers—when they are truly lovers and not just partners joined for the purpose of reaching certain goals—goes far beyond satisfying certain sexual desires, establishing a happy family or even reaching certain comfortable standards of life. It encompasses the basic longings. It goes beyond our own person, our own ego. As the poet Manfred Hausmann has put it: "It's a question of an experiment made magic, . . . trying to reach that which is beyond reality. This is an experiment doomed to failure and yet it's always attempted again and again with the courage and persistence of despair."

The desire to grow beyond ourselves as individuals, seen in the union of man and woman, is placed in our hearts by God himself. In the second chapter of Genesis we read that God made woman out of one of the ribs of the first man. Adam was jubilant when he recognized Eve and said, "This at last is bone of my bones and flesh of my flesh." But she is part of him as a woman and not as a second man, not as a buddy, a comrade or even as a friend. The woman is a part of the man, and yet she has her own identity. She is related to him, and yet she is completely different. She is his closest confidant, and yet she is a stranger to him. And the great longing of man and woman which God has placed in them goes in the direction of completing one another.

A wife suffers greatly when her husband seems to find his greatest satisfaction in goals that are so much less than hers. A husband suffers greatly because he feels inadequate to reach the total oneness which is the great yearning of his wife. And so he resigns, he gives up the struggle and takes refuge among other men—in his factory, on the football field, at the office, maybe even in the army. As Schiller says, "On the battlefield, a man is still worth something. There his heart is still weighed."

When his heart is put on the scale by the woman, it is always found too light. And that is why he feels like a schoolboy with a note on his report card reading, "Unsatisfactory."

The whole world acclaims his victories and his superiority. But when he has to face his wife, the man feels inferior.

# *The Inferior Man*

Even if men might call me crazy or declare war on me, I maintain that every man, if he's really honest, feels inferior to a woman deep down in his heart.

In Africa they tell the story about the chief who called all his men to come to his palaver hut in the center of the village. It was his fear, he said to them, that there were no longer any real men in his village. He had the impression that his men were being ruled too much by their wives. To find out if this were true, he asked all the men who felt that their wives bossed them around to leave the hut through the door on the right. Those who felt that they were in charge at home should leave through the door on the left. Lo and behold, all the chief's men left through the door on the right—except one.

So the chief called his men together again and gave a speech of praise to the lone wolf. "At least we have one *real* man in our village," he said. "Could you please share with us your secret?"

The man looked rather sheepish and at last, he said, "Chief, when I left home this morning, my wife said to me: 'Husband, never follow the crowd!'"

Where does this feeling of being subject to the woman, of being inferior to her, come from? I think it goes together with the fact that a woman has a gift which the man may have too, but in a much lesser degree. I'm talking about the gift of intuition. She seems to know things from the inside, intuitively, without thinking or mulling it over a long time. It's her heart which determines her decisions. While a man says, "This is what I think," she is apt to say, "This is what I feel." She is superior because she does not need to think things over. Of course, this is relative. There are men who are gifted with intuition just as there are women who have little of it. I have observed too that often the more emancipated a woman is, the poorer she may become in this gift. But on the whole, I think we are safe in saying that intuition is more a gift of women than of men.

When we have an important decision to make in our marriage, I take a piece of paper and draw a line in the middle from top to bottom. Then on the right side I write down all the reasons for the decision and on the left side, all the reasons against it. After hours and sometimes days of turning it over in my mind, I still don't know what we should do. Then one day my wife comes into my study with that certain shining look in her eyes and she says, "You know what we should do? We should accept that invitation," or, "How about doing it this way?" In the almost thirty years of our marriage I have never yet found her to be fundamentally wrong.

It is experiences like this which give a man the feeling of inferiority. In spite of long thought about a problem, he does not reach the quick conclusion which his wife does seemingly without thinking. He cannot trust his intellect in the same way that his wife can trust her feelings. Because he doesn't trust his own feelings, he is suspicious of the intellect of his wife. And this distrust makes him even more unsure of himself.

Even on a physical level a man feels he cannot compete. A man often gets less attention paid to his appearance than a woman. When you meet a couple on the street or look at a wedding picture in the window of a photography studio, a woman always looks first at the other woman. And the man? Naturally, he looks first at the woman. There is certainly something true in the expression "the fair sex."

Maybe this feeling of inferiority can also be explained by what he experiences sexually and how he experiences it. At least at the beginning of a marriage, a husband usually reaches a climax and achieves sexual pleasure much easier and more quickly than his wife. And just this taking, "free of charge," gives us men the feeling of being cheap. We must admit too that it's possible for us to gain sexual satisfaction without inwardly participating, without personal dedication and even without the investment of our feelings. At the same time we turn physically to a woman, we can still remain turned inwardly toward ourselves.

Zoologists tell us that in the animal world, sexual pleasure is only recognizable in the male of the species. In contrast to his wife, a man feels he is at a lower level, yes, even animallike, and that in turn makes him feel inferior. This feeling can make us unhappy although we are simultaneously experiencing sexual pleasure. We suspect too that while we can separate sexual pleasure and love, this is foreign to the deepest feeling of a woman. While the man can satisfy his sexual desire in intercourse without love, for the woman this is usually impossible.

On the other hand, in spite of the great love in his heart, a man may be incapable of uniting physically with his wife. However, it is always possible for a woman to unite with her husband physically even when she feels no love. We husbands have to reach that stage in love where the wife who loves has been from the beginning. She is miles ahead of us, and we come limping behind her. I am convinced that this difference is the main reason why a man feels inferior to a woman.

# The Fearful Man

Every man has had a negative experience with a woman at one time in his life. That was before his birth when he was the prisoner of a woman. For nine months before *she* gave birth to him he was contained within her body. Passive and defenseless he was born and delivered up into the hands of the woman who gave him birth.

Perhaps an unborn child doesn't feel like he's imprisoned. And yet unconsciously the man, more it seems than a woman, carries this memory within himself so much that it is often reflected in his dreams. I think many men live in constant, if subtle, fear that they might end up being such prisoners again. Of course a healthy relationship with a mother who does not smother but is willing to let go can offset this fear. Otherwise it may become the root of many conflicts later in marriage.

A husband comes home from work and his wife holds up a list of things that need to be done. The faucet is dripping here and a screw is loose there. The kitchen drain is stopped up and the basement fuse is burned out. He gets the feeling that his wife would like to take complete possession of him and boss him around. Fear swells up in his heart, the fear that he's in danger of losing his freedom. So he reacts negatively, even with hostility.

His wife is completely baffled by this reaction. She has no idea that her harmless request has awakened his old fear— the original fear of men toward women, the anxiety that someone is going to take possession of him, overcome him and even do violence to him. She almost becomes to him an impersonal force vying for control of his life.

A German theologian and psychoanalyst, Rudolf Affemann, says the same thing. "The woman is more of a unity (body and soul) than the man; therefore, it is her desire not only to love him completely, but also to possess him for herself alone. This desire makes a man feel very uncomfortable. He already has the deep-rooted fear within him (though he might not admit it) that the woman will rob him of his independence. Perhaps this is the fear which is an echo of his unconscious consciousness that she already possessed him completely at one time, namely in those months before birth."

A deep-rooted fear that he doesn't want to admit, an unconscious consciousness—these paradoxical expressions show how he is torn apart. They expose the inner conflicts under which the man suffers and which, because he cannot solve the problem, frustrate him.

But before I say more about the man who feels frustrated, I would like to consider the man who suffers because he feels superfluous, a feeling that is only strengthened by his frustration.

# *The Superfluous Man*

Strangely enough, a man gets the feeling that he is superfluous at the moment in which a new dimension is added to his manhood, namely, when he becomes a father.

The first major crisis in marriage often happens at the birth of the first child. It is the child who becomes the center of the mother's life. So the father can't help but feel superfluous, unnecessary and even like a pain in the neck.

When the first joy of his wife's announcement that she is going to have a child has faded away, then he realizes suddenly that he is only a helpless spectator, standing by during the whole process. All during his wife's pregnancy he can never quite get rid of this feeling. No matter how much he loves his wife and cares for her welfare and even shares her hopes and joyful expectancy, he still is unable to carry that unborn child.

Then comes the hour of birth. He spends it perhaps anxiously in the waiting room, left alone, sent out of the delivery room. A man never feels more superfluous, more cowardly, more castrated. It is another man or woman who is there to receive his child into the world. A nurse is taking care of his wife. He has no role to play. He is often not even allowed to be a spectator in this theater of life.

This waiting-room experience is so painful for him because it underlines a fact that he can't deny: he can never give birth to a child. After he has begotten the child, he is no longer needed. He has fulfilled his biological function. Now they can get along without him.

Just as he cannot give birth to his child, neither can he give his child its first nourishment. He has to stand on the sidelines and watch while his wife breast-feeds the baby. Again he feels superfluous.

He also feels superfluous when he faces his teen-ager. As his children go through puberty, they need him in a difficult double role. On the one hand they need him as their ideal, their mentor, the one with whom they can identify, on whom they lean and toward whom they struggle. But on the other hand he is their opposite, almost an adversary against whom they have to revolt, from whom they have to separate to find their own way of life, to become individuals. (The word *individual* means that which cannot be divided.)

It is a very difficult double role. The father must be like the strong pole or stake to which a young tree is bound when it is planted. The purpose of the stake is to keep the little tree growing in the right direction, so it will not be swayed to one side or grow crooked. The stake also protects the little tree from strong winds which otherwise might break it off. But the time comes when being tied to the stake is like being bound by chains. The cords rub deep into the tender bark of the tree and actually hinder its growth. The cords must be cut. The tree has to grow alone without the father stake. When that happens, the stake stands beside it feeling unneeded and superfluous.

This process is natural and necessary if the young tree is to grow properly. And when a father sees that his teenagers can get along without him, he suffers. This suffering is compounded because the protest of the young tree is misunderstood. It is not directed against the stake, the father pole. Rather it is a protest against the cords being tied too tightly or for too long.

The father's role is made even more difficult today because the authority of fathers is ridiculed and the purpose of the stake is put down. How often do we see in our society that the father stake breaks down, so that the children can neither wind around it nor climb up on it? Neither can they do battle with it so they can grow stronger. The father is not respected. He is even despised. Because he is not feared and respected, he doesn't dare to give any advice. He sinks down into meaninglessness.

Thus the father feels almost mortally wounded as a man. This time of breaking away seems to cause him greater suffering than his wife. Even in this situation she is more able to exercise her motherly functions of feeding and clothing and caring for the physical needs of her children than he as a man is able to exercise his fatherly functions. She who has a greater bond with the physical has other reserves from which to nourish her self-esteem.

It is no wonder then that the man who feels superfluous also feels frustrated.

# *The Frustrated Man*

The word *frustrated* comes from the Latin word *frustra* which means "in vain." In other words, one who is frustrated is one who feels that all he does is in vain. In spite of putting his whole strength into a project, he does not reach his goal, and he feels that everything he begins fails. A sense of inner helplessness overcomes him when he looks at the challenges which face him.

This feeling of frustration can be strongest sexually. Nothing hits him harder, is more crushing or painful to his inner feelings, than feeling himself a failure in the sexual realm.

He feels like a bull when his sexual urge is so strong that he can barely keep it restrained. Instead of being happy about this "strength," he rather feels ashamed. It makes him impatient, desirous, unreasonable, even brutal. The fact that sexual longing can overcome him without any deep feeling or inner participation, without tenderness and love and the atmosphere that goes with it, makes him feel base and animallike.

It is even more frustrating for a man if he has an experience of impotence—the other end of the scale—so that instead of feeling like a bull, he feels like a dishrag. Probably nothing in a man's life is more humiliating or shaming for him, nothing makes him feel less like a man, than when, in spite of his great desire and deep-felt longing, he cannot fulfill the expectations which he and his wife have in their sexual union.

I am now coming to a very difficult subject, but I don't

dare jump over it or ignore it if I want to put a man's sufferings into words and help his wife to understand him. We're talking about the peculiar and complicated relationship which a man has with his penis.

Again I will take refuge in the words of a poet. It is the gift as well as the task of the poet to put that which is almost inexpressible in human life into words. Johann Wolfgang Goethe wrote a long narrative poem entitled *Das Tagebuch (The Journal)* in 1810. But Goethe kept the manuscript a secret so that it was only published after his death.

*The Journal* tells the story of a married man who is on his way home after a long journey. It was his habit to write down the events of the day in his journal every evening "in order to give joy to his beloved." Unexpectedly, on the last day of his journey, one of the wagon wheels of his stagecoach breaks down and he is forced to stay overnight in a little village inn. While he is seated at the table in his room, writing in his journal, the maid, a young woman of great beauty, enters and serves him his evening meal. As he watches her skillfully setting the table and serving him, he finds himself suddenly overtaken by sexual longing. So he invites her to come back to his room when her work is finished. The girl, who has never slept with a man and who tells him that she is shy and reserved and has a very modest reputation in the village, decides, nonetheless, to return at midnight.

As he waits for her to come back, he finds to his consternation that his longing dies down. Whether it is because he enjoyed the anticipation more than the prospect of the event itself, whether unconsciously he is thinking of his wife and his faithfulness to her, or whether it is the purity of the girl which arouses guilt in him, when she does slip into his room at midnight and he feels her expectations as a duty, he cannot unite with her. He finds himself impotent.

In the meantime, the girl falls asleep in his arms, seemingly completely happy. "For her, it seems all she wanted was a sweet word, a kiss. That's all her heart was after." He lies awake beside her, angry at himself and putting himself down.

Then suddenly, as he remembers the first time he saw his wife and memories of his wedding and honeymoon fill his thoughts, he finds that he is no longer impotent. Now he would be able to have intercourse with the girl, but he deliberately chooses not to. They separate the next morning. He gets in the stagecoach, which has been repaired, and "comforted in heart," he lets himself be carried to the one he loves the most, his wife.

The poem ends with the lines:

There are two levers in the world
    which keep the earth's gears going:
The lever of duty is the one,
    but how much greater the lever of love.

In the course of the poem Goethe did something very bold. He gave the masculine genital organ a poetic name, since there was no other word that pleased him. He used the Latin word *Iste* which really means "This" in the sense of a pronoun. It enabled him as the one speaking to have a certain distance from "Iste," so he could talk with "This" in the familiar "Thou" form in German.

Goethe was unique in the use of this word, thus enabling him to express in words the strange and peculiar relationship of a man to his penis. In contrast to the woman who feels at one with her sexual organs—they are a part of her—the man stands opposite his, as if it were another person, a stranger. The woman *is* her organ. The man *has* his.

In Goethe's poem the word *Iste* is presented sometimes as the master and sometimes as the servant. But regardless in which role Iste appears, whether as master or servant, the man can't depend completely on either one. In either role Iste is self-willed. Iste is his own man and is not subservient to the will of his owner. And there we have the problem.

As master, Iste masters the man, and usually at the most embarrassing moments. Then in the right moment Iste can leave the man in the lurch. As love's servant, it is true, Iste does serve him. But often when the servant is needed, it may be that he refuses to obey.

And just that is the great suffering of the man. It is "not being able to count on" Iste. The man who likes so much to plan ahead, to figure out, to calculate, who likes to conquer and to have at his disposal, who gets his security in the feeling of certainty that he can manage everything: here he must remain dependent upon a self-willed servant and a moody master.

I don't know if a woman can ever completely understand this frustration. She cannot be left in the lurch by her sexual organ in the same way that the man can. Maybe she has no feeling (this is her great suffering), but still the sexual union can take place. Her inner readiness and the natural lubrication of the vagina which results from this readiness are not in the same measure a prerequisite of intercourse as is a man's erection. That's why we don't speak of impotence (inability to perform) when we talk of the woman, but of frigidity (inability to feel).

In the strict sense of the word, a man can be impotent—and that is what is so uncanny—in spite of deep feelings. Yes, it can even happen just because of his great longing.

"A woman will never quite understand him—ever." If

Tucholsky is right when he says this, then a man is defenseless when he has to face deep injury and hurt.

# The Vulnerable Man

Dr. Paul Popenoe, one of America's pioneer marriage
counselors, often said, "Men are hard, but brittle. Women
are soft, but tough." Perhaps this is true physically as well
as emotionally.

When we lived in a very difficult tropical climate, I was
ill more often than my wife. Especially during that time of
life when she was either an expectant or nursing mother,
she seemed to have unlimited powers of resistance to ill-
ness, which I, just then, in my feeling of masculine super-
fluity, did not have. It seemed too that when a missionary
couple had to go home because of health reasons, it was
mostly because of the husband.

Dr. Popenoe's statement would certainly be true in the
emotional realm. I believe that a man can be more easily
hurt inwardly and mortally wounded in his heart than can
a woman. Suicide rates for men are higher than for women.
A woman seems to have greater powers of resistance too in
coping with grief. After all I have said in this book, I have
no doubt, and perhaps you will agree that the ego of a man
is more fragile than that of a woman.

But how can we adequately explain a man's deep vulnerability? Shouldn't he be man enough, have the courage
simply to be the one he really is? Why does he have such a

hard time accepting himself as one who feels insecure and inadequate, helpless and fearful, unnecessary and frustrated? It is manly to face reality fearlessly and courageously, to call things by their name.

The problem is this: reality doesn't mesh with the image the world has of "The Man." The world's picture is a dream image, a cliché which can't stand up to reality. We all like clichés. Films with their heroes and heroines, villains, poor young girls, chauffeurs, detectives—they usually bring their producers money. The films which get away from these standard roles find fewer viewers. And yet there are some courageous producers who are not afraid to create such films. We need to become the courageous directors of our own lives.

A man is so vulnerable because he has to play a role which he is not able to play. Imagine that a well-known tenor who sings in a regional opera has to change his role and sing bass because his colleague has suddenly become ill. As a tenor he is used to getting hearty applause. And he feels sure of himself as a tenor because he has trained for this role and has spent long hours rehearsing it. He has mastered it. But now he stands on the stage and is supposed to sing bass. He's uncertain of himself and there's no applause, just polite coughing and murmuring. His pride is deeply wounded, and he swears he will never again take a role which doesn't fit him, even if the director should get down on his knees and beg.

The role which we men cannot play comfortably is that of being the strong sex. We strain and strain at it and still our performance is not very credible. We may have illusions about ourselves in our early years, but later in our marriages we find that we cannot earn much applause for our efforts. The real woman sees through such pretentions and would like to ask her husband to be just a kind human being and not some sort of superman. Not as Tucholsky says in his poem, to be "a man—and that's enough," but to be a person who knows his weaknesses, can stand up to them and is willing to share them with his wife.

Are we afraid to do this? Do we think that our wives would no longer love us if they could see us as we really are? What kind of love is that which is not centered on the real you but rather on a dream image which the partner thinks you are? Dr. Affemann has said it well when he writes, "To love is a continuing process of facing disillusionment and disappointment in the other one. This task has to be faced anew every day. Only in this way will the relationship of love be close to reality. True happiness is not built on false images, but on truth." Most women I know would much rather face this task than put up with a man who pretends to be satisfied with himself while playing a false role.

Love sees the other one as he is and accepts him that way. Love means too that I can let myself be seen by my partner as I am and be accepted that way. Because of our vanity this may seem impossible, but it would be a way of healing the vulnerability of the man if he would deliver himself up just the way he is to the love of his wife.

But what does he do? He defends himself because he's afraid of being hurt. Because he feels so threatened, the suffering man now becomes the man who reacts and his last resort is adultery, unfaithfulness.

# Two
## The Man Reacts

When one who is weak defends himself, he usually does it by pretending to be strong. The peacock, a delicate and vulnerable animal, displays its tail feathers to scare away opponents. The strength a man pretends to have is nothing more than the self-protective action of one who is unsure of himself and who is frightened. It's his way of defending himself when he is threatened.

There are two kinds of defense: a counterattack or a retreat into an impervious fortress. Men use both kinds. Even in the second defense they succeed masterfully in maintaining their manly image, even when they flee.

# *The Almighty Patriarch*

A patriarch defends himself through counterattack.

I have already mentioned the deep-rooted fear which a man has, but which he doesn't readily admit, that his wife could in some way rob him of his freedom. Because he is afraid of being possessed, he declares his wife to be his own private possession with him alone controlling the rights over her. He tries to reduce her to a thing so he is not threatened.

At the same time, this meets his urge to possess that which he has already conquered. He does not want to fight for ground that he has already won, to see his territory always put in question. Some even quote a Bible passage as the pious justification of a man's desire to possess once and for all that which he has won: "What therefore God has joined together, let not man put asunder" (Mt 19:6).

My wife and I were fortunate to live for several years in a region in Africa where we were not only the first Christians but also the first whites. There we could experience African society in its natural state. It helped me to understand in a new way many of my own unconscious but basic ideas.

In Africa the relationship of a man to his wife was often similar to that of a gardener to his garden. A garden's value depends on the seed the gardener sows in it and the fruit that grows out of it. If the garden bears no fruit, then there is no reason the gardener should not get rid of it and buy a new one. Let us carry this idea into marriage. If a wife has no children, then her husband can divorce her or take a second wife.

Divorce, polygamy and the choice of a partner therefore

are the exclusive privilege of the man. Yes, he may even commit adultery (sowing his seed in foreign gardens), and he wouldn't hurt his own garden by doing that. On the other hand, his own garden would become guilty if it allowed foreign seed to be sown in it. This pattern of thinking has created the double moral code which makes women more guilty than men if they commit sexual sins.

The patriarch is also the ruling father. That is why he has to be the superior one, the strong one—at least the stronger one. This often takes grotesque forms. In one of her books, Christa Meves, a well-known German psychologist and a Christian, calls these bogus patriarchs "ones who play God," "slave holders," "women keepers," people who reduce women to the status of temple prostitutes. Through this wrong picture of women, this distorted image, one can better understand the women's liberation movement.

Who would dream that a man does all this because he is afraid, because he has his back against the wall? It is just a defense mechanism, a camouflage, a mask behind which a man hides his weaknesses and uncertainty. Does a patriarch pretend to be the almighty one, the omnipotent one, to cover up his insufficiency, his impotence, in the broad as well as the narrow sense of the word?

Sad to say, this defensive action against an imaginary enemy takes place in many Christian marriages because a Bible verse is not quoted in its entirety and is taken out of context. "Wives, be subject to your husbands" (Eph 5:22). I am always a little suspicious when I see this is one of the few Bible verses that most men know by heart. Out of it they draw the conclusion that the subjection of the wife is one of the main characteristics of a Christian marriage. I will come back to this later. At this point suffice it to say that this interpretation is wrong.

The man who has to use a Bible verse to secure his advantage and as a camouflage must be very unsure of himself! He is living in permanent anxiety that someone is going to tear the mask away from his face. But he has more than one weapon at his disposal: he can also keep his distance and not allow anyone to get close to him.

# The Unapproachable Chief

In Africa we lived in the territory of six-foot six-inch Chief Rey Bouba. He rarely left his palace. Most of his subjects had never seen him. It was difficult to get past all his guards and have an audience with him. And those who did could only approach him with bowed heads and their eyes on the ground.

When we visited him, we had to cross an open courtyard covered with white gravel, so that we were blinded by the bright sunlight. In the semidarkness of his throne room he was encased in white cloths which covered both his body and his head. All we could see was the slit for his eyes.

A man enjoys being inaccessible, untouchable.

Once Chief Rey Bouba was sick and thought he was going to die. He sent for me and asked me to give him a penicillin shot. I can still see him whimpering in front of me, as with great delight I punctured the soap bubble of his unapproachableness.

To be unapproachable is just another defensive weapon

of the Chief. It enables him to escape in honor when he feels inadequate.

I found this unapproachableness in Africa especially among fathers in relation to their daughters. This is true elsewhere as well. Just read Johanna's letter to her father in chapter ten of my book *Living with Unfulfilled Desires*. Here was a girl completely cut off from a father she longed to express love to. But he could not receive it or express any to her. And often a woman finds the same pattern of unapproachability in her husband who has simply copied the example he has seen in his own father.

The Chief is not ready to talk. That is the complaint of countless wives. First they get married so they won't be alone, and then they want to get divorced for the very same reason. As Louis Evely, a French priest, has said, "Some women become widows on their wedding day."

Husbands will complain to me, "My wife always wants to talk things over." But we receive letters from wives, unhappy in their marriages, that often read like this: "I've been married for eight years. I'm really not unhappy as a wife and homemaker, and yet I'm in deep trouble. I often have a great desire just to talk to my husband, to experience things with him. But I sometimes think I won't even be able to talk to myself, I'm so out of practice. My husband does take me along at times to lectures and conferences, and we hear a lot of good thoughts. But we don't discuss them afterward and digest them at home, or even put them into practice. He can talk to others and carry on deep conversations. Sometimes that makes me mad, but I don't dare vent my wrath for fear that he will explode. That's when the tears start coming, and then he turns his resentments into complete silence."

Thus the unapproachable Chief often becomes the silent Buddha.

# *The Silent Buddha*

The reason men don't talk is the same reason they retreat into a shell where they can't be touched: they feel threatened, and to ward off attack they retreat into a fortress of silence, so that the blows miss their goal.

The more a wife tries to aggravate her husband—often the only way to get a reaction out of him at all—the more he withdraws and hovers like a silent Buddha above everything.

He already feels nagged and criticized by her simple request for time to have a talk. He doesn't think that his weak ego can take it.

Counselors of all kinds confirm the fact that more women than men come to them seeking help. From my point of view, one explanation is that because a man's ego is weak, he is afraid his self-image will be destroyed if he reveals that he needs help and must seek counsel. His manly desire to do everything himself would be spoiled if he has to go to someone looking for help.

Have you heard of the man who came home radiant after visiting his psychiatrist despite having postponed the visit a long time? He had wanted to get treatment for his inferiority complex. The doctor had healed him on the spot, he reported to his wife.

"How did he do that?" she asked.

"He simply told me that I don't have an inferiority complex. I *am* inferior."

If a man feels confirmed in his own diagnosis, then that's already as good as therapy for him. When he knows why he's sick, he already feels better. But that's not enough for his wife. She wants the therapy as well as the diagnosis. She would like to have her tears wiped away when she cries.

A man's retreat into silence also goes along with what I have already mentioned about his lack of intuition compared to his wife. To cover up the sense of helplessness, yes, even of inferiority, which he feels when he has to make a decision, he becomes silent. This reaction, or lack of action, can make his wife angry. It is true she doesn't want to be ruled by her husband, but she would like him to take the lead. She wants to be guided, but how can he do this if he won't talk? He is afraid of making a wrong decision which would expose his helplessness. To accept justified criticism, to admit his mistakes, this is more than his weak ego can take. If he doesn't say anything, then at least he can't say anything wrong.

## The Frozen Iceberg

Naturally a man's uncertainty in making decisions is intertwined with his uncertainty in the realm of feelings. If he can't reach a conclusion with his great intellect and logic, then he certainly can't rely on his feelings either—at least not in the same measure as women who have only to dip into their reservoirs of intuition. He simply has no confidence in his feelings because he usually lacks a certainty of instinct.

When he sees that he can't help his wife, that he can't give her what she needs, he retreats. He simply says that a true man does not rely on his feelings, as if not having feelings would be a virtue. Feelings are unmanly, he would say, effeminate, not part of being a real man.

It's not clear whether this role of the unfeeling man is exaggerated and put on, or whether the uncovering of his poverty of feeling simply adds to it. They probably both work together, augmenting each other.

We must differentiate between the inability to have feelings and the inability to show feelings. Just as I am convinced that there is no really frigid woman, so I am convinced that there is no really unfeeling man. If a woman is cold, it's probably because she's had to put her feelings in the deepfreeze to keep from hurting so much. And the same is no doubt true for the man.

That's why I don't speak about the man who has no feelings but about the unfeeling man. He can't feel his feelings anymore. Because he doesn't want them to show, he's locked them up in the basement. He's out of touch with his feelings. They are beyond his reach. Even if he wanted to, he couldn't put his hands on them.

The more a man tries to control his feelings, the more they control him. But on the outside we see the cold man who sleeps soundly, snoring away, while his wife cries softly beside him, longing for tenderness. He can't be tender because he thinks a real man is not supposed to be tender. And so he draws the conclusion that Christian Morgenstern, a German poet, expresses: "You can't be something which you're not supposed to be."

Maybe when he showed his real feelings once, he was deeply wounded. He may have heard in his childhood, "A boy doesn't cry." And so he learned, "When I show feelings, then I will be wounded. Therefore, I will show no feelings."

But this unfeeling iceberg is not the real man. It's just the way he reacts. His coldness is his defense mechanism—his safe shelter into which he can withdraw and achieve a certain invulnerability.

# The Man's Man

Hardly realizing it, in my description of how a man reacts to his inner pain and suffering, I have moved from his forms of defense to how he beats his retreat.

Today it is the woman who has come forth to counter-attack. She no longer lets herself be possessed. She puts her right to possess along with that of her husband. But this leaves only one escape route for the man.

Dr. Rudolf Affemann describes this phenomenon thus: "When the wife confronts her husband with her total rights of possession, then he can only flee to the rear. Either he stays at home and tries to flee inwardly (his professional interests, his study-den, his newspaper, television, hobbies) or he chooses to flee in activities outside his home."

To this flight outside his home belong the men's club, the soccer, baseball and football games, yes, even the sauna. He escapes back to his own sex. Here he feels like someone. He feels adequate as a man. He is among his own. He is no longer overdemanded, threatened by that which is strange to him. Here he can leave all his fears and anxieties behind. Here he feels understood.

In reality this is a sign that he has gotten stuck in the homoerotical stage of development (see our book *My Beautiful Feeling,* pp. 31-33) in which the ego is not yet strong enough to stand up under the complete differences of the opposite sex. It is more comfortable with the known aspects of same-sex friends. Marriage thrives on polarity, and it is only out of these opposite magnetic poles that it can keep on growing until the parting of death. If a man enters matrimony without being mature enough to stand up under this tension, then he is constantly tempted to fall back into the homoerotical phase, to flee to the sameness of his own sex, so that he may even look for a male sex partner. There's no doubt in my mind that the growing rate of homosexuality in our times has one of its decisive roots in this fact.

Men with fragile egos are too weak to stand up against the strangeness of what is different, what is foreign to their thinking, even uncanny. They do not go forth to learn to face fear, but they retreat to avoid fear. They do not dare to love. They even try to fool themselves and others that being together with other men all the time is very masculine. They can even appear to onlookers as the "strong ones" by using a raw form of voice and speech as they tell certain kinds of jokes among themselves, especially in the locker room and men's sauna. Here, surrounded by so much naked and anonymous manliness, a man feels secure and warm. He doesn't even realize it himself and certainly never would admit it, but this escape is in reality an expression of his weakness. It's a warding off of fear, fleeing to a place where there are no tensions.

As I write this, I think again of those words of Goethe's Faust as he took his walk on Easter Sunday.

Old winter, his strength almost gone,

Withdraws into the rugged hills
And from them, fleeing, sends back weak
Sleet showers that speckle the green plain.
(Randall Jarrell, trans. [New York: Farrar, Straus &
Giroux, 1976], p. 47.)

Helplessly, out of his helplessness, he sends showers of cold feelings over the greening meadows of feminine feelings. May this little literary association make the bridge now to the sexual sphere.

# The Tired Man

There are two shields of defense against the frustration men suffer when they know they can't rely on their sexual strength—tiredness and unfaithfulness.

"You are always so tired," is the reproach so often heard from wives. "Do you feel like it tonight, or should I take a sleeping pill?" the wife asks her husband in the American comedy *Mary, Mary* by Jean Kerr. It was meant to be funny, but the mingled response of the theater audience showed how true it was.

I mentioned earlier that a man is torn between two extremes—he feels either like a bull or a dishrag. He feels like the first when he makes use of his sexual powers without participating emotionally. He feels like a dishrag when despite the longing of his heart he is unable to have an erection and thus be physically united with his wife. In both cases he loses his self-respect and self-esteem.

As his shield of defense, he pleads tiredness. It's not difficult here to find good and plausible reasons for being tired: his job, his overdemanding profession, his countless other duties in the community, his failing health.

It's not difficult to understand his fleeing into tiredness. There is hardly anything else that a man is more afraid of than impotence. There is nothing which shames him more. Nothing makes him feel less like a man—even the guilt of infidelity. That's why if he is not completely sure of himself, he'd rather not even try. He prefers to say he is tired than risk the agony of failure.

He feels like a failure too if he is unable to bring his wife to complete sexual fulfillment. To do this he knows he must be one with her in his heart and have the emotional strength to express deep tenderness. But he fears failure. So to keep from getting hurt, he renounces their physical union and pleads tiredness—even though he is full of desire.

This does not mean that he is necessarily pretending to be emotionally tired or even using it as a cheap excuse. Emotional tiredness is not the same as emotional laziness. We must simply keep in mind that a man has a harder time finding his feelings. It takes longer for him to bring them out of his basement. Feelings cost him more strength. It takes him more time to get started, especially when he comes home at night after a hard day's work which he has only survived by repressing all his feelings. After keeping them harnessed all day, he simply doesn't have the energy to automatically release them again. He really is tired—both physically and emotionally.

Keeping in mind the biological fact that during sexual union the man is actually expending energy and giving of his substance, it is not surprising when after a day full of hard work he prefers to avoid further exertion. In addition, a French study has shown that the male sex hormone, testosterone, is at its lowest level in the blood stream at 11:00 P.M. and at its highest level at 8:00 A.M. The effects of this would be most pronounced in a man who is a lark who likes to go to bed early and get up early. If his wife is an owl who has just the opposite rhythm, certain tensions between them come into focus.

Though more research is needed, it is possible too that a man not only has a daily rhythm but also a monthly rhythm or cycle—times in which he has more and times in which he has less sexual desire. If this is true, then a woman on the pill who is sexually more available than before can be over-demanding sexually on her husband. This can be a secondary cause for impotence.

Certainly a man who is tired does not feel very manly. But it would seem more honorable to be tired than to be a sexual failure.

By being "tired" he has chosen the smaller evil. He longs for affirmation as a man. He would find it hard to live without the certainty of his potency. If he does not find this affirmation with his own wife, then he will look for it from another. Instead of facing up to shame, he would rather run away into guilt.

# The Unfaithful Man

Now I hesitate again.

When I began writing about the frustrated man, I was

afraid I might offend some readers by describing an occur-
rence which might be shocking. On the other hand, I was
afraid that I might lose other readers by trying elegantly
to avoid the issue. Again the poet of love from Weimar,
Goethe, comes to my rescue.

I would like to describe the unfaithfulness of the husband as his last resort—his last means of escape. Some of
you may throw up your hands and say: Whoever describes
adultery as a last resort—a way of escape—is defending it
and is trying to arouse sympathy for the unfaithful husband instead of feeling for the wife he has run away from,
has left behind. Other readers might say just the opposite:
After you've made a laughingstock of us men, now you are
starting to shake your finger in reproach.

This book was not written to make men look ridiculous
—neither to condemn them nor to justify them. It was written in order to understand them. I wanted to help men
who feel misunderstood and to help them understand
themselves. It is also my hope that some of those wives who
sigh in resignation or who are shocked by what I say will
begin to understand. Changing begins when one understands. The diagnosis is the first step to healing.

To write about infidelity in marriage is to write about a
fact. As far back as the Kinsey report in 1953, we could read
that half of all American men who had reached the age of
forty had had extramarital experiences. Three-fourths of
all the men questioned in the Kinsey study admitted their
wish for such experiences. I imagine that in the three
decades since that study was made, these figures have risen
even higher. When I was talking recently with a group of
young people, one of the students said, "Out of one hundred men, at least one hundred fifteen of them are unfaithful." The truth probably lies somewhere between Kinsey's

statistics and this rather contemptuous statement. Be that as it may, to write about the unfaithfulness of the husband as if it were abnormal would be pure hypocrisy.

I believe men tend to be unfaithful not because of weak character but because it is their last resort in the struggle to escape shame and pain. But now I ask, of the seventy-five per cent to one hundred fifteen per cent who may long for infidelity or even practice it openly without feeling guilty, do they do this only because they are afraid they might become impotent? If adultery is openly shown in so many magazines, books, films, television programs, plays and radio shows where it may either be glorified or made light of and where *faithfulness* is like a word from bygone days, then there must be a deeper reason.

Let's go back once more to Goethe's *The Journal*. You recall the man tells how he was forced to interrupt his homeward journey because of a broken wheel. He has found a place to stay overnight in a village inn. With love that is longing and full of desire, he thinks of his wife, who is waiting for him at home. At that moment a maid enters his room bringing him his evening meal:

She goes and she comes; I speak, she answers.
    With every word she seems more desirable.
And how easily she slices the chicken for me,
    Skillfully and more skillfully moving her hand and
      arm.
. . . It's all I can take, I'm lost, I'm crazy.
    With a desirous look I take in her tall form.
She bends over to me; I put my arms around her.

At the beginning the man certainly didn't have anything like this in his mind. But as the Germans say, *Gelegenheit macht Diebe*. "An open door may tempt a saint." "Opportunity makes a thief," and it also makes love. The adventure comes closer, prickling, enticing. The man is no longer capable of thinking reasonably and so he grasps.

What has happened here? We won't be able to understand it unless we look at the beginning of the poem. The traveler has just experienced a disappointment. His carriage had to be repaired and his long-awaited homecoming delayed. He was sentenced to boredom, passivity. "What can I do to make the time go faster but to grumble and murmur?"

The entrance of the attractive young woman into his room, her evident willingness, lets him know with lightning speed: here I can make up for my disappointment through a successful experience. Here I can overcome my boring passivity with a thrilling, quickly passing activity. The break in faithfulness will make up for the break in the wagon wheel.

With penetrating clarity one of the roots of masculine infidelity is laid bare here. Adultery is the escape of the disappointed man. His disappointment in this case has nothing to do with his marriage. In his genial manner Goethe puts into words what psychoanalysis has affirmed in the meantime. Many men who pretend that their strong sexual desires push them to extramarital sexual activity actually are suffering without realizing it because their ambitions and hopes in other realms have been unfulfilled.

For those who are disappointed in their marriages, this is the route of escape, now more than ever. They do not see themselves as strong husbands, but as uncertain and incapable, as helpless and superfluous, frustrated and vulnerable. Because of all this suffering they feel completely misunderstood. So they try to overcome their disappointment by reacting: by being the almighty patriarch, the unapproachable chief, the silent Buddha or the frozen iceberg. And when being a man's man fails as well as their escape into tiredness, when none of these things help, then the last resort is adultery.

The other root of infidelity, which Goethe's *Journal* makes very visible, is the desire for *Geborgenheit,* that wonderful German word which means more than shelter, refuge and security all in one. *Geborgenheit* is the foundation on which marriage stands. It comes from the word *bergen* which means "to rescue," "to bring into a safe place." *Burg,* the German word for fortress, stronghold, castle, means therefore the secure place where you have nothing to fear. In a marriage which is alive, each marriage partner feels secure, has no fear, is at rest with the other because each is convinced that his or her spouse wants only the best for the other. Does a husband give his wife this *Geborgenheit?* Does a husband find this feeling of shelter when he is with his wife? Where it is lacking, it can be his fault. It can also be her fault, but mostly both partners are guilty in not providing it.

In *The Journal,* the husband cannot be with his wife, and so he does not have this longed-for feeling of shelter. This is the same situation a traveling salesman has to face, a convention visitor, a soldier, yes, even a patient convalescing in a health sanatorium.

The man who feels unsheltered will be tempted to commit infidelity. Meeting another partner, regardless in which form this may happen, will be a substitute for this shelter. It is his last hope for security. So he looks for the warm, sheltering arms of understanding sympathy and affirmation.

There is still a third motive for adultery. We don't find it in Goethe's *Journal* but in another verse he has written. I would like to quote again from the first part of *Faust* where

Faust is taking a walk on Easter Sunday.
> Out of the stuffiness of the garret,
> Out of the squash of the narrow streets,
> Out of the churches' reverend night—
> One and all have been raised to light. . . .
> Already I hear the hum of the village,
> Here is the plain man's real heaven—
> Great and small in a riot of fun;
> Here I'm a man—and dare to be one.
> (Louis Macneice, trans. [New York: Oxford, 1951], p. 36.)

Everything which should give him the feeling of being sheltered—the coziness of his home, the security of a place to work, yes, even his church—this person now feels, perceives, as a musty prison, as a place where he's strangled, pressed down. He can't quite breathe. Goethe was certainly not thinking of marriage when he wrote this verse, but don't we find similarity to marriage in this picture?

A marriage which from all appearances is standing on the firm ground of shelteredness might not give this feeling at all but rather just the opposite. It's more like a torturing cord which strangles the persons in it. The one who feels bound up cannot blossom, cannot grow and develop. Rather he feels hindered by the squeezing narrowness of his marriage. There is a special kind of freedom which husband and wife mutually give to each other because they belong unconditionally to each other and are consecrated to each other, which makes them wonderfully free. Dr. Theodore Bovet of Switzerland has often said, "Without freedom, there is no genuine love." If this freedom is denied one to the other, then in its place there is distrust, suspicion, and everything is carefully calculated instead. Then all the man can do is to try to break loose from the "musty rooms" and look outside, beyond the gates of marriage for an encounter where he can finally say, "Here I am a person—here I can dare to be myself!"

In his adventure of adultery the man is looking for some kind of festive splendor which has been lost in his monotonous, everyday marriage—an "Easter Sunday walk," a "resurrection" which will stir him emotionally, intellectually and arouse at the same time his masculine power of potency. He is tired of eating dark bread at home all the time. He would like to enjoy cheesecake or a cream puff once in a while.

Adultery is the last resort of the suffering and reacting man. Do you feel understood by this interpretation?

But let me say one more thing to you. You are chasing after an illusion.

There was once a very gifted king in Bavaria, Ludwig the Second. He was a lonely and misunderstood man. He did not find the happiness marriage could have brought him with a loving wife. He tried to escape from reality into a world of his dreams. So he built himself a fairy tale castle in the midst of a wonderful landscape. He decorated his dream castle with art treasures from all over the world. Whenever he sat at his desk he could look at the beautiful tapestries and paintings of lovely life-size, feminine forms. But they only decorated the walls. They were without life and without warmth. It was only a dream.

It took seventeen years to build the fairy tale castle Neuschwanstein. For one hundred thirty-eight days, the king lived in this beautiful splendor. Then he disappeared mysteriously and was found in a mountain lake.

He who searches for unfaithfulness, the adventure of adultery, is like the king who tried to flee into the fairy tale castle. Meeting a partner outside of marriage can be so wonderfully beautiful in the imagination. But the one who tries it is living under an illusion. In marriage one discovers his partner as she really is, and there one finds the true balance between the dream picture of the emotions and the real person. Reality is denied in the adventure of adultery. One remains intentionally blind so the fire of passion will not go out, so the charm and appeal to the senses of the dream person will not dim. One lives only in the dreams that are painted on the walls of one's consciousness. It is a joy that is mixed with anxiety, the fear that these dreams will one day be uncovered as sweet illusions.

A man might experience an affirmation of his potency when he looks at the beautiful naked forms painted on the wall or when he leafs through a pornographic magazine. But in the deceptive phantom of infidelity he will look in vain for the healing of his disappointments, for true shelter and freedom. Indeed, on top of all the burdens he is already carrying and under which he is suffering will come the additional burden of leading a double life, one for his wife and one for his mistress. Adultery must always show two faces. He dare not forget to put on the right mask at the right place.

Unfaithfulness as a way of escape is a dead end. One can only feel sorry for the man who is trying to find his happiness and healing by resorting to it.

And yet there is true help for the one who suffers in himself and in his marriage. There is a way out, and we will talk about it in the last section.

# Three
## The Free Man

I intentionally did not entitle the third part of this book "The Ideal Man" or "The Man Who Is Human" or even "The Man As He Should Be." If I had done that, I might have put on already overburdened men even more demands that would have increased their frustration. By laying before them higher ideals, I might have made men feel more like failures, tempting them to give up completely. The result might be discouragement, even despair.

What I have described in the foregoing pages is the psychological reality of how a man suffers and how he reacts when he hurts. But no man will be helped if I just offer a few psychological tips. That would be too easy an answer.

Instead, a man must be set free, released, redeemed.

How does this occur? Through faith.

Faith is the act of jumping. I jump because I am pushed by logic and pulled by One who longs to catch me. It takes great courage to make this leap. It means springing over a deep abyss in confidence that there is One awaiting me on the other side.

All that I say in the rest of this book, I say out of my experience as one who has been caught. If you have not had this experience, it may be difficult for you to understand. But I hope I will not lose those readers, nor that they will be discouraged from reading further. Instead I want to invite and challenge you to take this leap. I would like to show you why it pays and how a whole new possibility of life is opened up to you if you dare to jump.

When I talk about this leap of faith, I am not talking about church membership or belonging to a religious fellowship. I am not talking about "churchianity" but about meeting God.

For the man who does not yet believe, the church is often like a wall separating him from God. For the man who goes to church only out of habit or tradition, the danger is that he may use this as a sort of bumper zone which protects him from having a personal confrontation with God on a first-name basis.

I have had this confrontation and I invite you to have it too. That's what I mean when I write the words *redeemed, set free.* It means being taken into a new reality. Let me illustrate.

There was a boy who walked by a pond every day on his way to school. During the winter the pond was frozen. His father had forbidden him to ever go out on the ice. But the boy did not obey. One day he ventured out on the frozen pond and fell through the ice. An old postman just happened to be walking by. He saw the boy drowning, hurried to him, grabbed his hand and pulled him out. He saved his life.

The boy had to stay in bed a long time. His father neither scolded nor punished him. When the boy was well again, his father took him by the hand and led him to the cemetery where he showed him the grave of the old mailman. He had saved the boy, but had to pay for it with his life.

The boy now knew: My life no longer belongs to me. I have received it anew and am alive because someone else gave his life for me.

This is what I mean when I talk about being caught. It is a passive experience. It may seem like the leap of faith is an activity, an action. It is, when you look at it from the point of view of the one who has jumped. But the one who is caught knows that he is caught even before he leaps.

So may the man who does not yet believe hear this personal question: Why should I not take this leap?

And the one who already believes should ask himself: Have I really dipped out all the rich possibilities that are mine since I have been caught?

# The Guided Man

In the previous pages I described how men react to their inner uncertainty by playing the almighty patriarch. Now is the time to show the other side of the picture and to spell out the characteristics of the free man, the man who has leaped and who has been caught.

First, he can lead others. Why? Because he himself is led. He has learned the secret of being guided. He is set free from the fear of failure because he no longer depends on his own strength but on the strength of his Lord.

With some men one can sense from the first encounter that they have learned the art of being guided by God. Others who call themselves Christians do not seem to have antennae for receiving his guidance.

Recently my wife was riding in a car with a friend in Washington, D.C., who was diligently looking for an address but who couldn't find it. Bill was an intelligent man, a capable man. He was the head of his department at the university where he teaches. But he wouldn't stop and ask for directions. Ingrid finally asked him, "Bill, why is it so hard for a man to ask directions? Women don't seem to have a problem with that."

His answer: "I never ask directions because I don't want to admit that I'm lost!"

There are records in military history of valiant cavalrymen plunging into the valley of death because they refused to ask if there wasn't some way around.

A redeemed man is one who is not afraid to ask for directions. In this way he leads. Only those who are led can lead.

How then can we be guided? Let me make a few suggestions.

First, guidance comes through the Scripture and listening prayer. King David said to his son Solomon as he was about to die: "I am about to go the way of all the earth. Be strong, and show yourself a man, and keep the charge of the LORD your God, walking in his ways and keeping his statutes, his commandments, his ordinances, and his testimonies, as it is written in the law of Moses, that you may prosper in all that you do and wherever you turn" (1 Kings

2:2-3). Our decisions must be weighed on the scale of his Word. Are they in accordance with the Ten Commandments? And then if instead of praying we become silent and listen, we will hear plainly the voice of the Good Shepherd, "This is the way. Follow me."

Second, guidance is often only clear when you take a concrete step in a certain direction. You can't steer a parked car. You have to put it into gear. A redeemed man has the courage to take this first step, and then he can hear a still, small voice which says, "Keep going; this is the right direction." Or he hears the voice saying, "Stop! You're going in the wrong direction."

In 1 Kings 19 we read the story of Elijah who was so afraid and depressed that he wanted to die, even after having a great victory for the Lord. God then speaks to him —not in a strong wind, not in an earthquake, not even through a fire, but through a sound of gentle stillness, a still, small voice. Outwardly, it could hardly be recognized, but inwardly, out of a quiet, receptive state, Elijah picks up the voice of his master and receives precise instructions.

Third, once this inner antenna has picked up the radio message there is only one thing left to do: obey without looking either to the right or the left, without being afraid of contrary winds. "He who observes the wind will not sow; and he who regards the clouds will not reap" (Eccles 11:4).

In his last book, written shortly before his death, Dr. Theodore Bovet of Switzerland said this about guidance: "When we listen to all the different inner voices, which often have to do with our whole life history, then we learn gradually to liken them to the needle of a compass or even better to the directions given by a radio tower to a landing airplane. We learn to listen quietly to the voice which says: 'Keep your hands off. This is not for you,' or 'Here's an open door, a real opportunity. This is a road your feet can travel.' "

Fourth, the art of being guided means also that you are ready to be corrected. My best friend told me once, "I'm even happy when I see that I'm wrong about something because that way I'm always learning something new." It's a very humbling experience, before God and before man, to have to admit, "I am wrong here. I have made a mistake." Accepting the humiliation of being corrected is a very painful learning process for us men. If we are on the wrong path, however, we should cut our losses instead of trying to cover them up and be overwhelmed by them.

This being corrected comes when we are in eye contact with God. His promise in Psalm 32:8 is "I will counsel you with my eye upon you." If we remain in eye contact with our Lord, he shows us the next step, but not the whole road.

I was reminded of this "eye contact" one day when working in the home of my oldest daughter. I had spread my papers out over the coffee table trying to make order in them when my little granddaughter came to "help" me. She was fascinated with the colored plastic folders and the papers each one contained, but before she touched them, she looked at me with questioning eyes. She was not yet two, but her sense of obedience was keen. "May I do this or must I leave it alone?" was what she asked me with her wide-awake eyes. I looked into them, nodding my permission. For a long time her little hands were occupied with making order.

Fifth, the experience of being guided includes also outward circumstances. Getting all the information together as well as the legal implications are a part of making a guided decision. I do not believe that a man can be "guided" and then deliberately do what is contrary to the law of the land in which he is living, provided that law is in harmony with God's law.

Sixth, we must not be afraid to make a decision. I have known many people who began to take the will of God seriously even in the smallest decisions. But soon they were living in constant fear of doing something that was not guided. They tried to press God's guidance into a single channel, and yet feared they would not find it.

A seminary student had a call to a small rural congregation and at the same time a call to work as a missionary overseas. He couldn't make a decision, so he went to the famous theologian Professor Schlatter in Tübingen and asked him which call was God's will. The professor's answer was short but clear: "Both."

We have a wrong view of God if we think guidance is bound to one track only. In the city of God there are many streets, all of which can be used. Often, of two possibilities both are God's will. Yes, I dare to say now and then we are allowed to decide simply according to what pleases us and causes us joy.

Lastly, the guided man also knows that God can write straight on crooked lines. He can even make something good out of our mistakes. His creative will is at work whether we are standing tall or have fallen flat.

Two people married too young without thinking through their decision. After a few years they realized they were incompatible and wanted to separate. But then they both had a personal encounter with God and made a new beginning together in faith. They discovered each other in a new light. Their love was resurrected and deepened in a way they had never before experienced. God made something much more beautiful out of their relationship than they had ever dreamed.

Knowing that God can make something good out of our wrong decisions takes away anxiety from the guided man and gives him courage to make decisions.

The strong, guided man is not tossed by the winds. He knows how to set his sails for the goal ahead and his sureness invites confidence. He is able to structure the unstructuredness of others while also knowing and accepting his own limits. He does not grieve over what is not given him, but dips out the possibilities and opportunities that are his. For this he needs humor.

# The Laughing Man

A man who has been set free to be a man, who has been redeemed, can be recognized by another special quality. He can laugh about himself. He doesn't need to prove himself by bragging about his accomplishments, like the man who feels inadequate. He is understated. He does not need to put all his certificates and degrees on the wall. He does not need to hide behind the mask of inaccessibility like the unapproachable chief.

Those who have dared to be caught by God expose their life to him. God's forgiveness helps heal the past. His nearness carries us now. His hands hold the future. This security gives the redeemed man a contagious, playful serenity

Instead of hurting others through sardonic humor or biting remarks, he encourages wholesome fun so members of his family and his coworkers don't take themselves too seriously. And if he hears a good joke about himself that hits the nail on the head, then he can laugh as heartily as his friends.

He can even laugh with his wife about sexual difficulties they may be having. Sexual demands lose their power to harm if a couple can have a playful conversation about them. A sexual relationship with no humor is like the animals'. God must love to hear the laughter of a couple behind closed doors.

If I am called to counsel a couple who are upset and who are constantly getting on each other's nerves, and I can get them to laugh about something together, then I know that the victory is already half won. Their marriage is in no immediate danger. I've often seen how just looking at wedding pictures can send a couple into gales of laughter. Memories long forgotten are recalled, and things that were painful at the time now seem so funny.

Humor helps us to live with situations which are unpleasant but which we cannot change.

My mother, who was a teacher with her whole heart and gifted in handling children, always said, "He who wants to learn must be happy." The atmosphere in a classroom often determines the success pupils will have. A relaxed atmosphere at the family table or in the congregation at church should also be highly appreciated. When I'm speaking some place and I can get my audience to laugh a couple of times, then I know that they will be more ready to swallow the hard words I will also have to speak. Those who take people too seriously, who think they are merely beings in need of moral or pedagogical change will not last long.

Loving little jokes help to affirm each other. As the proverb says, "The one who teases also loves."

In our family we have nicknames for each other, and for

special occasions we would make up funny songs to cele-
brate each one. When our youngest daughter was small,
she was delighted when I made up a song using her nick-
name. We had to sing it at our family table over and over
again to her. It made her feel accepted. It affirmed her individuality.

"Humor is a friendly chuckle about the peculiarities of
everything human," says Guardini. "It helps us to be merci-
ful, for after a good laugh, then everything is easier to
take."

Humor means that while you recognize the worth and
importance of all, just as they are, you also keep an eye open
for the peculiarities that they might develop.

The redeemed man is one who not only can laugh about
his inadequacies but who can also talk about them.


# The Talking Man

There is only one way out for the man who feels misunderstood and helpless, yes, even inferior, and who because of
these feelings tries to hide behind the wall of silence. The
way out is to talk, to communicate. The man who is ready to
say what's on his mind and heart is redeemed from being
the silent Buddha. He is ready to step out in front of his
walls of silence instead of hiding behind them with his hurt
feelings.

Because he is not afraid of his feelings, he can talk about
them. He knows that truth always brings freedom. "The

truth will make you free," Jesus said (Jn 8:32).

The redeemed man is also not afraid to face the feelings of others. He can accept his wife with her sometimes unreasonable longings and desires. If she is honest in expressing her true feelings, he can say, "I understand," without feeling either threatened or attacked. He knows that feelings are neither right nor wrong; they just are.

Because he has the courage to talk about his feelings, he discovers that many of his anxieties disappear. It is fear-reducing to put into words what troubles him. I think of the honesty of the psalmist when he says to his Lord: "I am in distress. . . . Set me free" (Ps 69:17-18) or in Psalm 32:3, 5: "When I kept silent, my bones wasted away through my groaning all day long. . . . Then I acknowledged my sin to you and did not cover up my iniquity . . . and you forgave the guilt of my sin" (NIV).

Man can talk because God has chosen him as his partner in talking. God takes his words seriously and thus makes man capable of dialog. We read in Hebrews 1:1-2, "In many and various ways, God *spoke* of old to our fathers by the prophets; but in these last days *he has spoken* to us by a Son." The redeemed man, the man set free to be a man, does not need to cover up his fears and let them grow under the surface until they come up again multiplied, which can lead to stomach ulcers or to heart attacks.

A redeemed man can take criticism and can talk it over. I remember as a young pastor in Germany, I was part of a team doing evangelistic work. After each series of meetings in a village, we had a time as a team to evaluate what had been done. Each one was allowed to tell the other team members what their gifts were, what dangers they faced and where they might have overstepped their limits. I found this honest sharing of criticism as well as praise most helpful in my personal growth. Criticism does hurt. Especially criticism that is true. We are all very sensitive about this. And I believe men are especially sensitive if they are criticized by women.

Before I was married I wrote to my fiancée a long list of what I expected from my future wife, and she wrote what she expected from her husband. The first sentence I wrote her was, "She must challenge me to the highest through absolute honest criticism of me." Then it continued, "When she is disappointed in me, she must never withdraw her confidence. . . . She must never pretend, but must tell me honestly when I have hurt her." I did not want a servant girl but an equal partner who stood by my side before God. Only with such a partner can a man become "one flesh"—a new, living being. Partnership includes the right to criticize.

Some men have difficulty accepting honest compliments and praise. I have often been comforted by the words of Paul in 1 Corinthians 4:5: "Judge nothing before the appointed time; wait till the Lord comes. He will bring to light what is hidden in darkness and will expose the motives of men's hearts. At that time each will receive *his praise from God*" (NIV). A redeemed man doesn't put himself down but can accept that God's creation of his uniqueness is good.

A redeemed man is also ready to listen in other ways. A theology student told me the other day that he was being kidded because he followed some good suggestions of his young wife. His answer to the teasing? "A smart man listens when his wife has a good idea."

A successful engineer, when asked the secret of his success in producing household machines, said: "I've always listened to my wife. She may not be always one hundred per cent right, but she's never wrong."

Such words begin to show the cycle of talking and listening and talking that is dialog. This is intimately tied to the sexual and emotional well-being of a marriage. Many men try to discover the secret of their wives' bodies, what turns them on, what makes them more ready at some times than others for the sexual embrace. It's not merely a matter of following steps 1, 2 and 3 like in a military manual or the handbook for some machine to get her to warm up. The greatest erogenous zone of a woman's body is her heart. And nothing touches her heart more than loving and affirming words that tell her she is loved. Biting, cynical remarks tear holes in the warm mantle of shelteredness which a husband's faithful love gives her. Icy winds then blow through these holes, and inwardly she becomes so cold that she cannot respond physically, emotionally, spiritually.

Marriage is not something static like a body at rest. It is not an achievement which is finished. It is dynamic, a process between two people, a relationship which is constantly being changed, which either grows or dies. Fuel has to be put on the fire, and that takes work. Healthy marriages take work too and dialog is part of that work.

Some years ago, after my wife and I had conducted a number of marriage seminars, we felt burned out. We were invited to participate in a Marriage Encounter weekend with twenty other couples of every age group. The newlyweds in our group found it hard to believe that those who had been married over thirty years still felt they had work to do on their own marriages. Three couples led the group. None of them were professional marrige counselors. They worked for a bank, a supermarket and a fire department. At the beginning of each session one of the couples shared in a personal but carefully prepared way the problems they had in their own marriage and how they had been helped through dialog. Two or three questions were then dictated to us. The women were sent to their rooms to write down the answers to the questions while the men went outside or into the library to do the same.

Twenty minutes later a bell sounded which meant that the husbands should join their wives in their private rooms. The notebooks were exchanged. Each one read what his or her partner had written, and then they discussed the answers for about twenty minutes. We heard the gong again and the whole group assembled in the living room. We began again with another of the leading couples telling of their experiences, giving us new questions and having us write down our answers.

The whole process was strenuous, often painful, but wonderfully healing. At the end of the weekend we discovered we had talked together longer and more in depth than we had been able to do all year. Without our even realizing it, our dialog had become superficial.

We found that writing down the answers to the questions was more helpful than merely talking. You have to endure without flinching what you see written on the page in front of you. You can't change it through a look or an inflection of the voice or even break it off when you see the other one is being hurt. Some of the questions we had to answer were: Why do I want to go on living? Why do I want to go on living with you? What are the things you have to put up with in me? What are the things I have to put up with in you? What is my main weakness and what is my main strength—as a man/woman, father/mother, Christian? How do I feel when I think about your death?

The man who has courage to dialog, to talk over these things, is a man who has been set free from his fortress of silence. And because he has been set free through Jesus Christ to talk, he is also set free to express his feelings.

# The Motherly Man

We have already looked at how we men tend to hide or deny our feelings because we think they are unmanly. The redeemed man is set free from this in a remarkable way. He is free to be motherly, to portray the tenderness of God.

The Kiga tribe in East Africa gives God the name of Biheko which means "a God who carries everyone on his back." In this tribe, only mothers and older sisters carry children on their backs while fathers never do. To portray Biheko, one of their artists made a wooden carving portraying a man who carries on his back a child with an adult face and in his arms a weaker child. This carving is a symbol of the God who takes care of human beings with the tender care of a mother. We see this God in Isaiah 46:3-4, "Hearken to me, O house of Jacob, all the remnant of the house of Israel, who have been borne by me from your birth, carried from the womb; even to your old age I am He, and to gray hairs I will carry you."

We are often not able to be in touch with our feelings because we think we must express everything objectively, without any feeling. But this is a sign that our spiritual lives are poverty stricken. We cannot mirror, cannot radiate the tenderness of God because we have not experienced it ourselves.

Yes, God is tender! The whole creation speaks of the tenderness of the Creator. The loveliness of the hills, the gentle flow of the streams, the light breeze blowing on our cheeks, the playfulness of the clouds—in all these there is a never-ending tenderness.

God is tender. As we read in Isaiah 25:8, he "will wipe away tears from all faces." And Revelation 21:4, "He will wipe every tear from their eyes, and death shall be no more, neither shall there be mourning nor crying nor pain."

What an unfathomable and yet fathomable tenderness lies in the fact that God became a child in Jesus. He became a person who could not only express his feelings of loving care, but he could also be the recipient of such feelings. He put all his love into a single glance when he looked upon the rich young ruler: "Jesus looked at him and loved him" (Mk 10:21 NIV). In modern language we would call it nonverbal communication.

Jesus was also not afraid to show his anger. In Mark 3:5 we read, "He looked around at [the Pharisees] with anger, grieved at their hardness of heart." He openly showed he was deeply upset about Lazarus's death: "When Jesus saw [Mary] weeping, and the Jews who came with her also weeping, he was deeply moved in spirit and troubled. . . . Jesus wept" (Jn 11:33, 35). He also cried over Jerusalem. "When he drew near and saw the city he wept over it" (Lk 19:41).

This Jesus who feels deeply is our example. But he is more than our model. For he lives in the redeemed man, conforming him to his image. The power of Christ within, not a man's own powers, sets him free not only to feel again his own feelings but also to feel the feelings of others. He can stand by their side as Christ would and with motherly tenderness dry away their tears with his big crumpled handkerchief.

Neither was Jesus afraid of physical touch. He held children close to him. He washed the feet of his disciples. John rested on his breast. He touched sick people and took the hands of the dead.

And he let himself be touched! A woman was allowed to

wash his feet with her tears and to dry them with her hair. "Standing behind him at his feet, weeping, she began to wet his feet with her tears, and wiped them with the hair of her head, and kissed his feet, and anointed them with the ointment" (Lk 7:38). Later he reproached his host Simon, "You gave me no kiss" (Lk 7:45). Jesus didn't even refuse the kiss of Judas.

God wants to be loved as a father and a mother are loved by their children, as a friend by a friend, as a man by his wife and a wife by her husband, as a sick person by a caring nurse and as a guest by his host. God finds great joy when we express our feelings toward him.

But before a man can feel his own feelings and express them, he often has to go back to the past and deal with that hurting child within himself, that frightened child, that hating child. Jesus loves all those wounded children in our hearts. He is the only one who is the same yesterday, today and forever, who can walk into our pasts, the time even before we were born, and place his healing and comforting hand on all those deeply sensitive spots that we try to cover up with the armor of our invulnerability. This wonderful healing of memories is the key to the man who has the courage to be motherly—the courage to express his deepest longings. This is the key to the redeemed man who, because the past hurts have been exposed to the Light and healed, no longer needs to retreat into his fortress, but stands there naked, vulnerable, ready to risk being wounded again. His fear is gone.

Is not this the deepest reason for our inability and our unwillingness to express feelings? Is it not the fear to expose ourselves to hurt? To show who we really are? We don't want anyone to see through us. We are not led by a spirit of love and confidence, but by a spirit of fear (2 Tim

1:7). This spirit of cowardliness leads us to great poverty. Then the things which we try to cover up in our hearts form the picture we have of ourselves. We become what we try to hide. Only what we can express and put into words will lead us out of the blocked-up feelings. Only what we share can be worked through.

We need spiritual help to overcome fear of people. This can only come through a living relationship with God: "If God is for us, who is against us? . . . It is God who justifies; who is to condemn?" (Rom 8:31, 33-34). Could it be that we are afraid to share our feelings with others because we have not shared them with God? We are not ready to be transparent before others because we have not been transparent before God? Yet he knows us already. "He knew all men" (Jn 2:25). He only waits for us to speak.

This inability to express feelings turns into guilt when we are so reserved that it destroys our fellowship with others, when we reproach others and even look down on them. We are not able to forgive or forget and therefore cannot radiate God's love and tenderness. "A happy heart makes the face cheerful" (Prov 15:13 NIV). Such a heart comes not from within ourselves but from a secure, open relationship with our God.

What are some characteristics of a man with such a relationship? The redeemed man is not ashamed to mourn, to grieve. All change can be a kind of loss—switching jobs, friends moving away, family problems, children beginning to leave the nest, losing his life partner. He needs to openly express his feelings of sadness and pain—of anger too.

All his life he has learned how to be a breadwinner, but does he know how to nurture the inner mind and heart of those entrusted to his care? He must give to his wife, his children and friends the room, the strength and the courage which they need to express their feelings.

Someone has suggested that women have fewer problems with aging than men since women are encouraged to express their feelings openly. Fear of aging stunts our growth. I think of the ninety-year-old German farmer who said, "The best lies yet ahead of us." Or as Robert Browning has written:

> Grow old along with me!
> The best is yet to be,
> The last of life, for which the first was made:
>
> Our times are in his hand
> Who saith "A Whole I planned,"
> Youth shows but half; trust God:
> See all, nor be afraid.

One of the secrets of the motherly man is the ability to put himself in the place of others. A Native American proverb says, "Don't judge a man until you have walked for a moon in his moccasins." Hebrews 13:3 encourages us similarly, "Remember those who are in prison, as though in prison with them." Jesus lived this truth for us as none other. "For we have not a high priest who is unable to sympathize with our weaknesses, but one who in every respect has been tempted as we are, yet without sin" (Heb 4:15). When he who is God became man, he "emptied himself, taking the form of a servant, being born in the likeness of men" (Phil 2:7). Jesus could feel what people felt because he did not remain aloof, a God untouched by human pain. He became one of us.

What about us? Paul says, "Have this mind among yourselves, which is yours in Christ Jesus" (Phil 2:5).

A freed man is also a good host. He anticipates the needs of his guests, provides for them, and puts their needs before his own. "Do not neglect to show hospitality to strangers, for thereby some have entertained angels unawares" (Heb 13:2).

Finally, motherliness in a freed man means giving affirmation. When I asked the wife of a redeemed man, a man whose very being radiates Christ, what she appreciated the most about him, she answered without hesitation, "He affirms those he meets." I believe when Jesus asked us to "clothe the naked" (and that certainly is a motherly task), he also meant to clothe those who feel stripped of their self-worth and self-esteem. Love is encouragement and kindness. "You can do it!" "I'm on your side." "I believe in you." Love is also the challenge, "Now do it!"

A redeemed, motherly man holds his wife securely in his arms, even when he does not know why she is crying. He spreads a blanket over her and sees that she is not cold. He stoops over to his child and takes him on his lap. The child is safe and can grow strong to meet the storms of life. Motherliness and fatherliness, both are attributes of God. The closer we come to him and perhaps the more mature we are, the more these attributes become one.

# The Fatherly Man

Men who feel superfluous at home are tempted in their pain to withdraw and flee to another place where they will find recognition. Recently I asked a young wife about her father. "I barely knew him," she said. "He left it to my mother to bring up nine children and told her, 'If I do nothing, then at least I do nothing wrong.' " Another young man said, "My father cannot show me his love, probably because he hurts so much himself."

A man who is set free to be a man, a redeemed man, can overcome his pain because of the affirmation and strength he has received from his heavenly Father. He can then give to others the fatherly love which he has experienced.

He is ready to share with his children, taking each one of them seriously and accepting their individuality. He also knows the secret of sharing his work with them. I recall that when we came home on furlough from our work in Africa, I was asked to give a missionary message in various congregations. My oldest son, Daniel, was my escort. Though only seven at the time, he felt very much a part of the team and would ask me, "Father, where are we going to preach next Sunday?" Solemnly he would take his place beside me at the front of the church and pray with me for the success of the message.

Later on when Ingrid and I were called to teach Family Life Seminars throughout the world, we tried when at all possible to have one of our children with us. Not only was it a special reward for all the sacrifices they had made in letting their parents go, but it was the only way they could know just what we had been doing in our teaching and counseling ministry. We felt that every cent we put into their travel costs was one of the best investments we could make.

But when does being a father begin? The chief of the Chaggas, a proud and industrious tribe living on the slopes of Mount Kilimanjaro, told his men, "Take good care of the pregnant woman. She is the most important person in our tribe." This wise African chief had long ago discovered what modern-day psychologists and psychiatrists are learning—that the acceptance of a child and the resulting self-image and self-esteem of that child begin long before birth. When a father knows that he is essential to the future well-being of his child, then he need never feel superfluous, especially when his child is unborn.

It is the strong, decisive, responsible, planning man who starts nurturing his wife so that she can become a good mother. He understands her in her cycle. His heart is filled with awe and wonder when he reflects that new life can come from the act of love. And that this new life is dependent on him, his protecting hand and loving care. He helps his wife in choosing a doctor who will not relieve him or rob him of his responsibility to coach his own baby's birth and will allow him to go to prenatal checkups. He stays at his wife's side at the birth of their child. He provides a safe environment and strong encouragement during the nursing period, taking an active interest in the child's daily development and growth. He is wide awake, anticipating the pitfalls and dangers that his children may face. Because of that, they can place their confidence in him. On the other hand, if a child disappoints him, his world does not crumble. He does not receive his identity from his children, but from the Father from whom every family in heaven and on earth is named.

Such a father is the hero for his four, five, six, seven-year-old child and older. When puberty comes, the child develops a strong desire toward independence, and even though he may find and seek outside heroes, the deep underlying knowledge is there: father is the best example to follow. By daring to take an active part in nurturing the whole family he has become the best example of a father. He has taught fatherliness to his sons and given his daughters the best guide for choosing a husband.

The fatherly man is patient. He has learned the secret of waiting. In the story of the prodigal son, the father let his son go—but he waited. Every day he waited. He gave his son freely of all for which he had worked, knowing that the son might waste it. The son didn't have to wait until the father died. He took his share of the inheritance and spent it on loose living. The son didn't even think what it might have cost his father—blood, sweat and tears. The son thought only, "It's my right!"

The father was relaxed about letting his son go. He knew that his son was no longer his problem but God's problem. He had given him his very best. I'm sure the father suffered pangs of not being needed, of being superfluous, but he stood up under this pain.

A few years ago I planted three birch trees in our front yard, thinking they would grow without help. At the first windstorm, one tree broke off, so I put up two poles for the others and fastened them securely to the poles. One of the poles was too strong. It was more like a fence post. Because it could not give at all, the top of the little tree bound to it broke off at the level of the post, so that today there is only a stump where there should have been a tree. But there was just the right amount of elasticity in the pole to which the third tree was bound, so that both could bend with the wind. The day came when the cords were untied and the tree stood proudly alone. It is developing evenly on all sides, and its growth is a joy to behold.

A son wrote to his father, "I'm moving out. I'm leaving home and leaving you. I, your son, am not 'at home' anymore with you. I'm leaving home for good. The prodigal son didn't receive any good advice, any commandments, any rules of what to do and what not to do. For me the time has come to leave father and mother." The young man left home and went to live with his girlfriend.

The father wrote back, "The son who goes away from home is not a lost son, not a prodigal son. For his father, he was never a prodigal son. This may be what the son thought as he took care of pigs in a faraway land. And it's not true that his father didn't give him any rules of behavior. Neither for the one who tells the story, Jesus, nor for those who listened was there any doubt that the way of living described in Luke 15:13 was not according to the will of the Father. Why did the son turn around if he had not been going in the wrong direction? There must have been a discussion which took place beforehand, which is not recounted in Luke 15."

It is the great ministry of the fatherly man not to give up, but to persevere. He has to offer resistance, so that his sons and daughters can grow up straight. He is a father, not only to his own physical children, but to the children of others who have no father who cares for them. It is not true that one must have wife and children in order to be fatherly. There are young men, not yet married, who are fatherly. There are priests, called to a celibate life, who are fathers for the family of God.

Where else can a man learn to be a father if not from the heavenly Father? "As a father has compassion on his children, so the LORD has compassion on those who fear him; for he knows how we are formed, he remembers that we are dust" (Ps 103:13 NIV).

The world is looking for redeemed men who have the courage to be fathers.

# *The Sheltered Man*

In contrast to the frustrated man who would like to run away from his responsibilities stands the redeemed man who feels safe and secure. He can be a shelter to others because he himself is sheltered. He is not afraid even if at times he should lose or suffer defeat. He simply gets up again and keeps on keeping on. He is a man that has accepted himself not only with his strengths but also with his weaknesses. His secret: he knows he has been accepted by the heavenly Father. He has a roof over his head. He knows where his home is. He has a place where he can put his feet under the table. He can say with the psalmist, "You prepare a table before me in the presence of my enemies" (Ps 23:5 NIV). He can say, "Thou art my refuge, a strong tower against the enemy. Let me dwell in thy tent for ever! Oh to be safe under the shelter of thy wings!" (Ps 61:3-4).

This is the longing of all mankind—to have security, to know where one's place is. God created man and then he created a place for him, the Garden of Eden. When man lost God, he lost at the same time his place. Since then, the longing for a place where he belongs, where he feels at home, is in the heart of every human being. Those who have not found a place, the uprooted, the eternal Gypsies will find a place nowhere, not even in marriage. On the other hand, those who have found a place, married or unmarried, will be able to become a place where others feel at home, thus filling one of the deepest needs of our time. In light of this, Jesus' promise "to prepare a place" for us is filled with new meaning (Jn 14:2). Those who have found him have found their place.

Perhaps the best symbol of the man who feels sheltered, safe and secure, is that of the tree described in Psalm 1. "He is like a tree planted by streams of water, that yields its fruit in its season, and its leaf does not wither. In all that he does, he prospers" (v. 3). In meditating on this verse and after observing a magnificent tree in all its autumn glory, I wrote these words down in my journal, "A tree rests. A tree stands firm because the roots are deep down. A tree drinks constantly. A tree supports, gives shelter, warmth, security. A tree bears fruit. A tree is not in a hurry. It waits for the right time."

The redeemed man, symbolized by this tree, is a whole man. He is whole first of all because he *belongs* to a family, the family of God. God, his Father, makes him one of his sons.

He is a whole man because he feels *worthy*. Christ died to give him birth and therefore he can take as his own the worthiness of Christ.

He is a whole man because he feels *competent*. This competence comes from the Holy Spirit. "God did not give us a spirit of timidity but a spirit of power and love and self-control" (2 Tim 1:7).

In front of our little mountain home in Austria stood an old bent and crooked fruit tree which belonged to one of our wonderful farmer neighbors. It had had to bear the brunt of the strong northwest wind, but it was a paradise for our children. They could climb it easily even before they started school. From this vantage point they could look down on the adults who might be around. A summer visitor looking carefully at the rugged tree asked Matthias, our neighbor, what kind of fruit could possibly grow on such a tree. Matthias answered with a twinkle in his eye, "Children." This tree is a symbol of the man who radiates security, who creates the room where others can be happy and prosper. Not like the father whose son said, "When Dad comes home, a dark shadow enters the house with him."

The man who is sheltered, who is safe and secure, is not afraid to lose his freedom by giving his time and strength to his family. He counts it sweet fortune to be a servant of love. He may have been hurt in many battles himself, but as Thornton Wilder says, "In love's service, only the wounded soldiers can serve."

On our mantlepiece we have a wooden sculpture depicting the Holy Family. Mary is seated holding the baby Jesus. Joseph stands behind her spreading out his warm cloak as if to protect her. One of our friends, Ruth Heil, who admired the sculpture, wrote the following about it in a letter to us. What better description could there be of the safe and secure man?

How wonderful to see the baby enclosed in the mother's arms and then the mother in turn protected and surrounded by the father's mantle of love. The father's protection is at the same time offering shelter and freedom, protected and yet wide open, a refuge in storms and yet challenging. This open cloak which shelters mother and child from the cold winds outside is held also by the guiding hand which lets the child go free. Because the child has been sheltered, he can also handle the responsibility of freedom. This cloak of protection, does it not also give the woman the freedom which she needs to move about and develop freely? Christ is the One who covers us and yet he does not strangle us in narrowness. He creates the place, the home, and leaves the door wide open so that we can go in and out.

The mother and child are a unity in themselves. Just

the two of them alone would be beautiful. But what would become of them if the wide cloak of the protector were not around them?

And the man alone with his arms outstretched? It's as if he's saying, "May I not give you protection?"

One is completed through the other. The child through the mother; the wife through her husband; and surrounding them all is the wide, invisible mantle of our heavenly Father, who enables them to develop and grow in the shade of his unending refuge which heals all of the torn places in our human mantles.

These torn places are often visible in the way that husband and wife express their sexuality. What freedom for a man to learn to take into account how he feels physically and put this into words, so that his wife knows that when he says he's tired, he is tired! He doesn't have to accept unconditionally all of her wishes and try to fulfill them when he knows it will lead to disappointment for her. Neither does she remain passive and silent when she is not ready to unite. A wife is not frigid because on some days she may not feel like having intercourse. And neither is he impotent if he has no desire for intercourse or may at times have the desire but not be able to have an erection.

What freedom when a couple is released from their need "to perform" and learns to enjoy the pleasures of relaxed, easy sex! They can then forget about being spectators, let go completely and enjoy their sensations. Physical love is the most intimate sphere in the life of a married couple. Every man is different. Every woman is different. Therefore, every couple is doubly different, and a part of the fun of sexual love is the originality of each couple.

When God created man in his own image, he created them as man and woman. He made Eve from the rib of her husband and brought her to him. Is there any better way to explain the great desire of husband and wife to become one flesh than that they came from one body?

"You are all around me on every side; you protect me with your power" (Ps 139:5 TEV). Because the redeemed man has experienced the love of God in his own life, he can give it to others. He knows that to love is a great risk, and he may be hurt, but he is willing to take this risk.

Ingrid and I know what the risk of loving means. We were separated by continents when we were engaged: she as a missionary teacher in Cameroun and I as a pastor in a large congregation in West Germany. Let me share what she wrote to me from her lonely station.

I want to tell you why I love you. When I picture you in my mind, I can see you stretching out your hand to me. I trust your hand for it is the hand of a safe and secure man. It is true, you walk a little ahead of me, but when you realize I'm getting out of breath and can't quite keep up, you stand still. You turn around and give me your hand to help me over the hard places. Then I come very near to you and you talk to me and comfort me. You don't make fun of my thoughts, neither are you threatened by them if they challenge you to try a new path.

When I am weak and need protection, I know that you are stronger than I, and so I take hold of your hand because I know that you will never use your strength to make me feel inferior.

But you need me too and you are not ashamed to show it. Even though you are strong and manly, you can also be helpless as a child. Your strong hand can then become an open, empty hand. And I know no greater happiness than to fill it.

# *The Loving Man*

He who loves is no longer alone. The one he loves is constantly present with him. He renounces the right to remain at the center of his own life. He permits someone else to enter into the midst of it and senses that to be sweet fortune. He gives himself up and lets himself go. He becomes empty like an open hand which holds nothing, but waits until something will be put into it. He who loves has the courage to become one who needs something.

I asked several of my good friends how they would describe the loving man. How does he show his love? Here are some of the answers:

Dieter Endres said, "The loving man is one who does not let the personality of his wife become stunted. At his side, she can blossom because he doesn't put her down. He helps her in a practical way to develop the gifts which God has given her to be used for his honor and for a blessing to the family, community and congregation."

Susanne, his wife, said simply, "He is the one who loves me, his wife."

A fatherly friend and counselor, Klaus Hess, said, "The loving man is not one who is seeking to be loved, but his great happiness is to give love. Then his wife can respond. That which you would like to receive, you must give. To win a whole heart means to give a whole life. Marriage, that close relationship to one woman, is a man's training ground. There he is allowed to practice and learn that which gives him authority for all other areas of his life and profession."

When I asked his wife, Amalia, she replied without a moment's hesitation: "For me, the loving man is the one who includes his wife in his work. He holds out to the end, through thick and thin, whether it's easy or hard, and gives unity with his wife top priority. Pain is often necessary to reach this unity. We must not try to avoid or run away from pain because marriage grows through crisis."

Herta Kosche said, "The loving man is the one who creates an atmosphere of shelter where we as a family can breathe deeply and be at rest. We have no fear. He does not bully his wife, nor wound her dignity."

One of Ingrid's sisters responded, "The loving man is the one for whom it is more important that I am happy than that he is happy."

Another friend said, "He's the man who likes his work, for if he doesn't like what he does, then he doesn't like who he is, and he can't love me."

In *A Growing Love,* our friend and poet Ulrich Schaffer writes,

> love never comes to stay
> it can't be stored for the future
> and past love does not answer to present needs
>
> love grows out of our experience with God
> love grows out of our acceptance of ourselves
> love grows out of our acceptance of each other.
> (New York: Harper & Row, 1977, p. 96.)

The title of a novel by Christian author Manfred Hausman, entitled *Liebende Leben von der Vergebung* (A Life of Loving out of Forgiveness), became a motto for Ingrid and me. For how can one live either singly or together without the grace of forgiveness? Our lives can be full of the goodness of the Lord if we are not afraid to admit and confess our own guilt. The banner of the forgiving love of the Crucified One stands over us to make us compassionate.

My Ethiopian friend Getahun put it this way at a marriage seminar he and his wife, Linda, were leading:

In Ephesians 5:21-33, the man has a far more difficult job than his wife. She is told to submit to him in verses 22 and 24 and to see that she respects him in verse 33. But for the loving husband there is a far greater program. He too must submit, verse 21, but then he must also be the head of his wife as Christ is the head of the church, in other words, her manager, verse 23; he must love his wife and be ready to die for her, verse 25. He must sanctify her, make her clean, wash her, see that she is radiant, that she has no stain, no wrinkle. He must love his wife as his own body, for "he who loves his wife loves himself," verse 28. He must never hate his wife, but nurture and care for her. He must leave everything else and cleave to his wife, verse 31.

As Getahun explained this, step by step, he was brave enough to admit that in Paul's fourteen-point program for husbands in Ephesians 5, he, after ten years of marriage, still had a long way to go. "Perhaps I have succeeded in the first two points," he said. "We men have a very big job."

Where does this leave the man? With a burden of being a loving man that is impossible to carry because only God can love completely? No. Rather it is the opposite. The man is not expected to love perfectly. God does that. This is a great relief. We can rest in him to fulfill the woman.

We are not, however, completely relieved of responsibility. While we cannot love totally, we can love truly. To the degree God has put love in our hearts for another, we can express that love in grace and truth. In this, being a loving man is not impossible. He can show her that she is loved through a kind word, help with an errand, a hand on the shoulder, rearranging a schedule to be with her.

The loving man is, therefore, the loved man, loved by the One who is love. He does not love out of his own strength. This is foremost in his mind and heart. Life is secondary in light of the hope of eternal life. Ultimately the man depends on God and can face, endure and enjoy life only because he is not dependent on this life. His wife and children mean more to him than any other human relationship and are second only to his relationship to Jesus Christ. He loves because he was first loved.

*Epilog*

It belongs to being redeemed—to be satisfied with the provisional, the temporary. Even if one never reaches the goal, it is good to be going in the right direction.

I was born in the next to the last hour of the next to the last day of the next to the last month of the year. This has been a paradigm for my life and a challenge to have the courage to accept incompleteness in this imperfect world.

Thus it is not my intention to give the last word on men in this book. Those who are only satisfied if they can write the last word will never write anything. In all of life—particularly where our ultimate goal is concerned—we must have the courage to accept incompleteness. For the basis on which we stand, from which we originate and out of which we live, we must have nothing but the ultimate completeness, the final reality.

Christ is the final reality. Everything else has only a shadow existence. His love penetrates us and radiates through us.

*Walter Trobisch*

## *Afterword*

My dear departed husband,

   More than three years have passed since you left us and
were catapulted from one moment to the next to your
heavenly home. This manuscript was on your desk—unfinished. While the first two parts on the suffering man and
how he reacts were quite complete in your handwriting,
the last section on the redeemed man, the freed man, was
only there in outline form with a few key words and sentences under each subtitle. Your friends and your children
helped me put the fragments together. I then tried to make
it a unity, using your own words and stories. I listened to
that still, small voice and then wrote it down, trying to keep
out of the way. It was my prayer that this would be your
book, your message to both men and women. If it is true, as

C. S. Lewis says, that in our grief we often take on some of
the characteristics of the one we mourn, then perhaps it is
"Walter in me" which speaks.

The last section on the loving man was the most difficult
one. In your notes were only three sentences:

"The loving man is the submissive man," and you wrote
the reference to Ephesians 5:21: "Be subject to one another out of reverence for Christ."

"The loving man *cleaves* to his wife." In German the word
*hangen* could mean "to be attached to" or "to hang on to."
You wrote, "The man is not independent, but dependent."
"For this reason a man shall leave his father and mother
and *be joined to* his wife."

I remember when I first knew that I could love you. We
had ridden through the Palitinate in southern Germany on
your motorcycle. It was a cold winter day in February 1950
with rain and sleet beating in our faces. When we reached
the parsonage where we were to stay overnight, the pastor's
wife gave us hot tea and made us take a warm footbath.
Then I was told to rest on the sofa until the evening meal.
You found a blanket, covered me and tucked it under my
feet. (Do you know that your sons do the same thing today?)
That blanket was a sign of your love, and under it I felt safe
and secure.

Today I want to thank you that in all the years of our
marriage you helped me establish the boundaries of my
daily life. When I shared with you the long list of things I
wanted to do in one day, you gently said, "It is too much.
Let's decide all the things you do *not* need to do today."

One of my friends described her husband as her chief
"caller forth." I could certainly say the same about you.
Often I would draw back and not want to take responsibility
for a new task, like that marriage seminar in Indonesia two

months before your death. You gave me a blessing and said, "You can do it, Ingrid." In every new venture that we felt was guided, you encouraged me. It wasn't always comfortable and I was often ready to give up. But it was good "survival training" for the time after your death. Since then I have often felt your hand on my shoulder saying: "Just one step at a time. Keep on keeping on. His strength is made perfect in our weakness." I remember too the many times we were separated in our marriage and how you said that you trusted me to make the right decisions and to act on my own in emergency situations.

I was never happier than when you said that you needed me, because often I felt that I was in your way. This was especially true when you were working on a manuscript. You were then the pregnant one. I could only stand by and wait patiently—sometimes not so patiently—for the baby to be born. After such a time you once wrote to me these words, "I sense how very much I need you as a woman, as a person, as nearness. I look forward to our being together again, and we will begin right away our dialog in depth. I need you so very much, above all, your trust, your patience, your presence."

I also thank you for being such a good father, not only for our own children, but for so many others who found healing in their heavenly Father because you stood as a bridge to help them find him. I know how you suffered too as a father. It was not easy for you to see your children cut the cords which bound them to the "father" pole and learn to stand up straight on their own. I just want to tell you that this pain which you endured has brought fruit. I want to thank you too for helping to heal that "fatherless" child in my own heart. Growing up without a father in my teen-age years left wounds which your patience helped to heal.

We had one great problem though. In spite of all these outward and inward signs, I sometimes found it hard to believe that you really loved me. When we were married in June 1952 in the Christus-Kirche in Mannheim, our chairs were far apart, a symbol of all that we would have to bridge in our marriage—two different mother tongues, traditions and geography. We both knew that neither of us was the "dream picture" that each had imagined as a partner. You even said laughingly but honestly that you would have liked a petite, dark-haired wife, and look what you got—a tall, red-headed Swedish-American! We knew beyond a doubt, though, that God had led us together and because you said yes to me, I could answer with my yes to you.

How often did it happen in our life together, that just when I was ready to answer your love, you turned and left and I could see only your back? Your self-discipline seemed to take over. I have never met a man who accomplished as much as you did in your fifty-five years on this earth. Your sense of duty was great—whether it was to answer the daily pile of mail on your desk, to finish your current manuscript, to help people in their spiritual lives and with their personal problems or to organize Family Life Seminars throughout the world. It seemed to me then that everything else was more important to you than our marriage. I looked at your back as you turned to your work and my heart would weep. You did say that you loved me, but so often I could not accept it because I had not yet accepted myself completely.

Over the years I learned too that it is hard for any man on this earth to come into those dark recesses of a woman's heart and fill all her needs. Only One can do that. It is, no doubt, the greatest anxiety that a woman has—to be unloved. If I could tell my sons only one thing about the loving man it would be this: he is the one who can give his wife the assurance that she is loved. He does not forget to tell her in some way every day that she is number one in his life. And she must hear and accept what he is saying, both in word and deed.

How often we said in our seminars, "You can never change your partner; you can only change yourself"! Remember when our niece wrote after years of struggle in her marriage, "Since I have accepted my husband as he is, instead of how I would like him to be, we have peace"? It was so much fun to go to our first Marriage Encounter back in 1975 after we had conducted a number of seminars for other couples. My love for you was very great as you dared to share out of the depth of your heart. I have the notebook in my hands where you answered the dialog questions we were given. In the same notebook I found the letter you wrote to me after our last training seminar in Ottmaring, Germany, when each person wrote a love letter to his or her partner which was then mailed a few days later. You ended your letter with these words:

My wish is only that also my admiration and joy, the warmth that I feel in my heart for you should reach you, lay hold of you and make you certain deep within of my love. I know that often I have not taken the trouble to tell you this, or I have not done it intensively enough and I ask you to forgive me and not to give up on me. I promise you that I will not give up on you either and that I will be faithful to you until death do us part and that I will fill up your cup with never-ending patience. Because it is only out of your filled cup that I can fill my empty sheets of paper with living words.

Each morning when we were at home, you would come into our bedroom with a tea tray. You were an early riser, a lark, and sometimes you had already written for two hours at your desk before it was even light. Deliberately and lovingly you then prepared a pot of tea and brought it to our room. After sharing it together we would read the Daily Texts according to the Moravian Church and plan our day together. Each morning as you did this loving service, I would think of how Jesus did the same for his disciples as we read in John 21. They had fished the whole night but without success. When it was morning, Jesus stood on the shore. He gave them explicit directions as to where they should cast their net. They were obedient and caught one hundred fifty-three fish. When they had pulled their net to shore and had got out on land, they saw a charcoal fire, with fish lying on it, and bread. Jesus had prepared a fire and breakfast for his tired, hungry and cold disciples.

And you did the same for me. When the door opened and I saw you with the tray, I could sense the presence of Jesus with you. We often discussed this and chose this text to be engraved on the family tombstone, "Just as day was breaking, Jesus stood on the beach" (Jn 21:4).

Then came your last morning, October 13, 1979. You had arisen early as usual, gone for your morning run, shaved and bathed. The door opened to our room and there you stood with the tea tray. It was your last deed on this earth—to fill my empty cup.

*Ingrid*

## Selected Bibliography

Affemann, R. *Geschlechtlichkeit und Geschlechtserziehung in der modernen Welt* [Sexuality and Sex Education in the Modern World]. Gütersloh: Gerd Mohn Verlag, 1979.

Bovet, Th. *Mensch sein* [Being Human]. Tübingen: Katzmann Verlag, 1979.

Illies, J. *Kulturbiologie des Menschen* [Human Cultural Biology]. Munich: R. Piper & Co. Verlag, 1978.

Meves, C. and Illies, J. *Lieben–was ist das?* [Loving—What's That?]. Freiburg: Herden-Verlag, 1970.

Schaffer, U. *A Growing Love*. New York: Harper & Row, 1977.

Tucholsky, K. *Ausgewählte Werke in zwei Bänden* [Selected Works in Two Volumes]. Reinbek bei Hamburg: Fritz Raddatz, Rowolth Verlag, 1965.

Unseld, S. *"Das Tagebuch" Goethes und Rilkes "Sieben Gedichte,"* [Goethe's "The Journal" and Rilke's "Seven Poems"], Insel Library Volume 1000. Frankfurt: Insel Verlag, 1978.